W9-DJE-290

SUICIDE
THE GAMBLE
WITH DEATH

GENE LESTER is Assistant Professor of Psychology at the State University College of New York at Buffalo. She has written numerous articles on the relationship of psychological development and death.

DAVID LESTER is Associate Professor at Richard Stockton State College, Pomona, New Jersey. In addition to writing many books and articles on the nature of suicide, he is a member of the Suicide Prevention and Crisis Service of Erie County, Inc.

SUICIDE
THE GAMBLE
WITH DEATH

GENE LESTER

DAVID LESTER

PRENTICE-HALL, INC. *Englewood Cliffs, New Jersey*

A SPECTRUM BOOK

Copyright © 1971 by PRENTICE-HALL, INC.,
Englewood Cliffs, New Jersey.

A SPECTRUM BOOK

Current printing (last number):

10   9   8   7   6   5

C–13-875823-9

P–13-875815-8

Library of Congress Catalog Card Number: 71-153444

Printed in the United States of America

PRENTICE-HALL INTERNATIONAL, INC. (*London*)
PRENTICE-HALL OF AUSTRALIA, PTY. LTD. (*Sydney*)
PRENTICE-HALL OF CANADA, LTD. (*Toronto*)
PRENTICE-HALL OF INDIA PRIVATE LIMITED (*New Delhi*)
PRENTICE-HALL OF JAPAN, INC. (*Tokyo*)

PREFACE

Intro

Suicidal behavior is an exceedingly serious problem. The rate of completed suicide over the nation as a whole is about 10 per 100,000 per year. In other words, in one year, 10 of every 100,000 people kill themselves. Multiply this by the appropriate number for your community and you will find out how many families are disrupted, how many lives prematurely ended by suicide. There are probably about 10 suicide attempts for every completed suicide, which adds up to 110 suicidal acts per 100,000 people every year. So ubiquitous is the impulse to suicide that about 50 percent of the students in a recent survey at the University of Maine had considered, threatened, or actually attempted suicide.

Aside from its effect on the suicidal person's community and family, the rate of suicidal behavior should disturb us all, because it is an index of unhappiness and emotional disorder. No one performs a suicidal act if his life is satisfactory to him. We should be concerned not only with the problem of understanding and preventing suicide, but also with the need for improving the quality of life as it is experienced by the unhappy person. Preventing a suicide is not necessarily a beneficent act if it forces the potential suicide to continue in a life of misery.

This book is directed toward increasing an understanding of the factors that cause suicide. We will present research evidence in a number of areas that are thought to be related to suicidal behavior. As the reader will see research in many of these areas is very difficult to do. For example, when we try to study hereditary factors in suicidal behavior, we cannot interbreed people deliberately as if they were fruitflies. We must settle for the matings that are decided by people's own choices. Of course, the results that we obtain will not be as clear-cut as those that come from deliberate experimental arrangements.

Research on suicide is further complicated because suicide is a complex behavior. Suicidal acts occur in different people who otherwise seem to have little in common. Consider, for example, these three cases of suicidal behavior:

1. An old man who finds that he has cancer and kills himself while he he is still strong.

2. A schizophrenic patient in a mental hospital who jumps out of a window while in an agitated state.

3. A housewife who takes ten aspirins after an argument with her husband.

These three people share very little except their suicidal behavior. In fact, the cases are so different that we suspect that there may be many kinds of behavior masquerading under the single label of suicide. At present, however, we cannot differentiate the behaviors very well.

The title of this book reveals a bias which will be present throughout the rest of the book. Although suicidal behavior may be irrational and illogical, it is nonetheless aimed at improving an unpleasant situation. The seriously suicidal person (like the rest of us) does not know what death is like; he risks disappointment, but hopes for triumph or contentment. The mildly suicidal person may hope his act will change his life, but he risks dying instead of awakening to an improved life. In addition to winning happiness or escaping from misery, the person may try suicide with the hope of preserving his threatened self-image. If he foresees severe illness, poverty, or mental disorder, he may use suicide to preserve the memory of himself as he was at his peak. This, again, is a gamble, especially since the disapproved act of suicide is likely to tarnish his image.

In all suicidal behavior, we feel, the element of ambivalence about death is crucial. The probability that death will occur varies depending on the method chosen, but it is rarely one hundred percent. The shotgun in the mouth may jam; the fall from a window may be broken by a tree; the poison may not have been correctly labeled. The choice of method, the time, and the place are all reflections of the person's degree of ambivalence, for they determine the probability that death will occur—the odds that the gamble will be won or lost.

A good example of the presence of ambivalence in suicide is found in the Tikopia of the South Pacific. Young people among the Tikopia commit suicide by swimming out to sea during the night. When they are missed in the morning, their neighbors get into boats and paddle after them. The potential suicides determine the probability of death by the time of night when they leave. If the suicidal person leaves the island long before dawn, he may have tired and drowned before he is reached. If he leaves soon before dawn, the oarsmen may overtake him and bring him back to land.

The gambling aspect of suicidal behavior also contains a strong fatalistic quality. Most people enjoy the experience of gambling at times —finding "what Fate intends for you" through the turn of a card or the fall of a die. When a person has reached intense despair and confusion, he may in some sense gamble with his life in order to find out what future is "determined" for him. The wife who takes an overdose in circumstances such that her husband may or may not find her may be hoping that Chance will determine her future. If he finds her and saves her, that is proof that he loves her, and her fate is to go on with a life that is worth living. If he does not save her, he does not love her, her life is not worth living, and death is the proper fate for her.

As a result of the problems we have mentioned—the complex nature of suicide, the difficulties of research on humans, and the ambivalence of the suicide himself—research on suicide is often open to criticism about its design. The interpretations drawn from specific results are also frequently open to question. In the course of this book, we will from time to time offer criticisms of the research we report. The reader, too, should keep an open and critical mind. To help him do so, we have provided a bibliography at the end of each chapter. The source of each study cited in the chapter is given in the bibliography, so the reader can check for himself on the results being reported.

For the reader who is not familiar with psychological and sociological research, we should give one word of explanation. In reporting the results of a study we will sometimes say that there was or was not a "significant" difference between numbers. This expression does not mean that the researcher decided on his own whim that the results were important or not. It means that a statistical calculation has shown that the results would occur accidentally only on very rare occasions. (However, readers and researchers alike must remember that those rare occasions sometimes happen!)

CONTENTS

SUICIDE
THE GAMBLE
WITH DEATH

CHAPTER 1

SUICIDE:
A MEANINGFUL
BEHAVIOR

A fifty-year-old man, George J., is despondent after losing his job. His wife criticizes his ability to make a living and threatens to leave him. He is concerned about a physical illness. One afternoon, he goes into the garage, cleans his shotgun, carefully closes the garage door, and shoots himself in the head. He dies instantly.

Another man, John M., of much the same age and circumstances, ties sticks of dynamite to his belt and blows himself up outside his house.

Most people, whether laymen, psychologists, or physicians, would agree that these two deaths were clear cases of suicide. They appear to fit the dictionary's definition of suicide as the act or an instance of taking one's own life voluntarily or intentionally.

A thirty-year-old woman, Martha S., learns that she has only a few years to live. She is unmarried, and her mother, to whom she was devoted, has recently died. She goes to her car in the garage, runs a hose from the exhaust pipe into the window, gets in, and starts the car. She also takes a number of sleeping pills. Just as she is losing consciousness, the meter-reader enters the garage on his way to an entrance to the basement. He pulls her out into the air and calls an ambulance. The woman does not die.

A married woman of twenty-five, Susan G., is annoyed with her husband's behavior and decides to teach him a lesson. He arrives home every day punctually at 5:00. At 4:30 she takes a large number of sleeping pills and lies down in the hallway of their house. The husband is injured in a traffic accident on the way home, and no one comes to the house until 9:00. The wife dies.

Which of these women has most in common with the first two cases mentioned? Martha S., who intended to die, lived, because of the intervention of someone who found her accidentally. Susan G., who intended only to frighten her husband, died.

It becomes clear that the fact of death produced by one's own voluntary act is not necessarily a sufficient criterion to use in judging whether a *psychological* process of suicide has occurred. The woman who meant to frighten her husband took the sleeping pills "voluntarily and intentionally," and her act resulted in her death. Is this the same kind of psychological process implied in "taking one's own life voluntarily and intentionally"? No; this particular case of self-destruction seems rather to be an accidental death following an act which was intended to be dramatic rather than deadly. Susan G. has in common with the male suicides mentioned above only the fact that she died.

Martha S., who did not die, actually appears to have more in common with George J. and John M. than Susan G. does. Martha, John, and George all had histories of recent loss and the threat of further unhappiness in the future. They all made specific and careful preparations for their suicidal acts; they chose relatively lethal methods. Only an accident prevented Martha from sharing with John and George the achievement of death.

These cases make it clear that an understanding of the suicide process can not be found simply by looking at the end state (death or life) of the person or at the person (whether the one who died or someone else) whose act brought about death. Nor do particular circumstances of life invariably produce suicidal acts. Many persons who find themselves in the straits of George, John, and Martha do not behave suicidally. Others kill themselves as a result of disturbance about events which would not be taken seriously by the majority of people. The process that leads to suicide can not be detected by looking at whether death actually occurred, nor by investigating whether a person's life was objectively miserable. Rather, the purpose of the suicidal act within the pattern of the individual's life must be examined.

In newspapers and magazines, the high incidence of suicide is often described with the words "suicide strikes 20,000 people in the course of a year," or "suicide is the fourth greatest killer of young people." The implications of these descriptions are wrong. Suicide does not "strike" in the sense that measles and tuberculosis strike. Suicide is the result of a gradual process within the individual rather than of a mysterious stroke of lightning from outside. The implication of the "suicide strikes" idea is understandably cherished by many persons because it helps them feel relieved of responsibility for the suicides of people close to them. They are allowed to feel that suicide can not be prevented or even predicted, and that the suicidal person is struck down by an incomprehensible blow like that which destroys the heroes of Greek tragedies. It is rather clear, however, that potential suicides give many warnings about their state of mind. Also, as we will note later, suicide is far more likely to occur in particular kinds of people than in the general population. To understand suicidal behavior and deal with it successfully, we must abandon the comfortable "suicide strikes" philosophy and examine the characteristics of suicidal people.

Actually, everyone has a theory (a set of beliefs) about suicide, although he may not be able to articulate it clearly. Along with the specific beliefs about suicides that exist in most people's minds is the idea that it is impossible to analyze or theorize about suicide. Unfortunately, many of the common sense beliefs about suicide are wrong and may be useless or even destructive in dealing with suicidal people. Edwin Shneidman, Norman Farberow, and Calista Leonard have compiled the following list of "facts and fables" about suicide:

These statements are NOT true	*These statements ARE true*
FABLE: People who talk about suicide don't commit suicide.	FACT: Of any ten people who kill themselves, eight have given definite warnings of their suicidal intentions. Suicide threats and attempts *must* be taken seriously.
FABLE: Suicide happens without warning.	FACT: Studies reveal that the suicidal person gives many clues and warnings regarding his suicidal intentions. Alertness to these cries for help may prevent suicidal behavior.
FABLE: Suicidal people are fully intent on dying.	FACT: Most suicidal people are undecided about living or dying, and they "gamble with death," leaving it to others to save them. Almost no one commits suicide without letting others know how he is feeling. Often this "cry for help" is given in "code." These distress signals can be used to save lives.

FABLE:
Once a person is suicidal, he is suicidal forever.

FACT:
Fortunately, individuals who wish to kill themselves are "suicidal" only for a limited period of time. If they are saved from self-destruction, they can go on to lead useful lives.

FABLE:
Improvement following a suicidal crisis means that the suicidal risk is over.

FACT:
Most suicides occur within three months after the beginning of "improvement," when the individual has the energy to put his morbid thoughts and feelings into effect. Relatives and physicians should be especially vigilant during this period.

FABLE:
Suicide strikes more often among the rich—or, conversely, it occurs more frequently among the poor.

FACT:
Suicide is neither the rich man's disease nor the poor man's curse. Suicide is very "democratic" and is represented proportionately among all levels of society.

FABLE:
Suicide is inherited or "runs in a family" (i.e., is genetically determined).

FACT:
Suicide does *not* run in families. It is an individual matter, and can be prevented.

FABLE:
All suicidal individuals are mentally ill, and suicide is always the act of a psychotic person.

FACT:
Studies of hundreds of genuine suicide notes indicate that although the suicidal person is extremely unhappy, he is not necessarily mentally ill. His overpowering unhappiness may result from a temporary emotional upset, a long and painful illness, or a complete loss of hope. It is circular reasoning to say that "suicide is an insane act," and therefore all suicidal people are psychotic.

Shneidman and his colleagues have suggested that there are four principal situations which give rise to a "suicidal crisis"—a period of time when a person seriously considers suicide because he feels that the pressures of life have become intolerable. The suicidal crisis may pass, but while it is present it is a very dangerous time. The four main kinds of suicidal crisis are these:

1. *Impulsive suicidal behavior* may follow anger, disappointment, or frustration. The emotional crisis may be highly temporary, but in an impulsive person it may lead to grave danger.

2. *The feeling that life is no longer worth living* may be the result of a serious depression and may lead to suicidal behavior. The person does not understand or believe that his feelings of worthlessness (of both himself and the world) will eventually go away. He may feel that he is seeing life as it really is, and that in his previous non-depressed phases he was deluded about what life had to offer.

3. *Very serious illness,* as in the case of Martha S., may lead to suicide as an escape from suffering or with the altruistic aim of sparing loved ones the difficulties of caring for the sick person during a long terminal illness. It should be noted that the suicidal person may not really be ill at all, but may simply believe that he is. As long as the belief is present, whether it is correct or not, the person may turn to suicide.

4. *"Communication" suicide attempts* may occur when a person does not really wish to die but wants to change the way other people act. Susan G.'s death occurred by accident in an attempt to communicate her annoyance to her husband. The suicide attempt may be intended as a way to punish others or to win their sympathy and interest. Often it has the opposite result and arouses hostility and guilt in people close to the attempter. The person who attempts suicide as a means of communication should not be ignored or despised because he is "only trying to get attention." His life has to be extremely unhappy for him to be forced into such a desperate measure. And, as with Susan G., there is some risk that he will actually die as a result of his "communication."

CLUES TO SUICIDE

Later in this book we will discuss the characteristics which make a person's suicide probable—for example, marital status and age. This information is essential to the understanding of suicide as a general form of behavior. However, most people at some time in their lives are concerned about the possibility that a specific individual will commit suicide. We stated earlier that suicide is the result of a gradual process rather than a bolt from the blue. What are some warning signals that such a process is going on?

First, of course, warning clues in the circumstances surrounding the person and in his general mood can be examined. Has he received a distressing frustration or disappointment recently? Is he depressed, or has he been in the recent past (remember that suicidal behavior is likely to occur after the "crisis" as well as during it)? Does he believe that he is seriously ill? Are his social relationships so confused and unsatisfying that he may attempt suicide in order to get a message through to other people?

Second, the person is very likely to give specific clues in his behavior. He may make statements that refer to his suicidal thoughts:

"My family would be better off without me."

"I'm going to end it all; I can't stand this any more."

"I won't be around much longer for you to put up with me."

"I don't want to be a burden."

"This is the last straw; this is all I needed."

"I can't stand it any longer: I want to die." (Shneidman, Farberow, and Leonard, 1965, p. 9)

Such statements may be made casually or in isolated moments by persons who do not go on to kill themselves. However, if a sick, unhappy, or depressed person makes remarks of this kind, people close to him should be alert to the possibility that his words are warnings of suicide. After a suicide has occurred, relatives armed with hindsight may recall many remarks which foreshadowed the death. They may then say that "of course, they couldn't have known he really meant it"; but a normally alert and sensitive person who knows the facts about suicidal behavior can recognize clues about suicidal intentions before it is too late.

In addition to the kinds of remarks discussed above, a suicidal person may show behaviors which involve planning for death: making a will; arranging insurance policies and business affairs; giving away cherished or valuable possessions. None of these *necessarily* implies suicidal intentions, since people with foresight generally do have wills and life insurance. However, if the person has been ill or depressed, if he has talked about death or prolonged absence, if he seems to be making arrangements to care for his family when he is gone, such behaviors may well be a further indication that suicide is about to occur.

If a person gives away objects that have been important to him (for example, skis or other sports equipment; tools needed for a trade or hobby), he may comment to the recipient that he (the giver) "won't be needing these any more." A warning signal like this could hardly be missed unless the friend was convinced that "those who talk about suicide don't do it."

More general changes in behavior may also precede suicide. The potential suicide may lose his appetite and his interest in sex. He may be unable to sleep well; early-morning sleeplessness is especially characteristic of depression. He may lose weight and show little interest in hobbies or social life.

RESEARCH INTO SUICIDE

It is clear that many clues can help to identify the suicidal person before his fatal act occurs. Recollection of these clues after a death can also help to identify the death as being due to suicide rather than accident or homicide. However, like any other human behavior, suicide comes in many different forms and can be extremely difficult to classify. This fact, along with others, makes suicide an area in which research is often complicated by methodological problems. Before we attempt to discuss particular areas in which research has given us some understanding of suicide, it might be well to warn the reader briefly about difficulties encountered by students of suicidal behavior.

1. Not all suicidal acts result in death. Attempted suicides and completed suicides should probably be regarded as different forms of behavior. (However, as was noted earlier, either an intended suicide attempt or an intended suicide completion may accidentally be turned into the alternative.) In addition, there are other minor forms of suicidal behavior, such as threats or thoughts of suicide.

2. The most valuable way of categorizing suicidal behavior probably involves the measurement of intent to die. Low intelligence or mental disturbance may render the individual unable to achieve his intent. However, measurement of intent is difficult, particularly if the person under investigation is already dead.

3. The degree of consciousness behind the suicidal act may be an important dimension. It is sometimes claimed that some people kill themselves in an "automatized" state (e.g., when they have already taken a lot of sleeping pills) such that they are not really aware of what they are doing. Some workers also feel that serious suicidal preoccupation can lead to automobile or other accidents in which the person is killed or hurt without consciously intending the event. Again, some long-term self-destructive behaviors, like alcoholism, are sometimes classed as unconscious suicide attempts.

4. Occasionally, individuals who kill themselves may be motivated other than by self-destructive urges. Males with disturbances of sexual behavior sometimes hang themselves briefly in order to achieve sexual orgasm. Several cases have been reported of boys who died in this way. Their motives were undoubtedly very complex, and perhaps should not be classified simply as suicidal.

5. When suicide is studied demographically rather than through individual cases, difficulties may arise because of incorrect classification of cause of death by coroners or physicians. Many social pressures cause the suicide's family to prefer the death listed as accidental rather than suicidal. Suicide is still frequently considered as "crazy" or indicative

of some moral degeneration. Some religious bodies will not grant full religious burial privileges to one who is labeled a suicide. Insurance policies often pay nothing to survivors if a death is due to suicide; on the contrary, they may pay double indemnity if the death is accidental. Thus, many deaths by suicide may be classed as accidents, giving an incorrect measurement of suicide rate. This fact is especially unfortunate for suicide research because particular kinds of people are more likely to be classed as suicides than others: the indigent or derelict is probably more often judged a suicide than is the "pillar of the community."

CONCLUSION

It is clear that suicide is not a simple problem. Many difficulties obscure comprehension of the behavior. On the other hand, suicide is not a "bolt from the blue." It occurs in some situations more than in others. People who are suicidal risks give warnings which can be recognized by those close to them. Suicidal behavior forms a logical pattern and is potentially understandable. The following chapters are devoted to some of the facts about suicidal behavior and some discussion of how this information can be used to prevent suicides.

BIBLIOGRAPHY

MENNINGER, K. A. 1938. *Man against himself.* New York: Harcourt Brace Jovanovich, Inc.

SHNEIDMAN, E. S., FARBEROW, N. L., and LEONARD, CALISTA. 1965. Some facts about suicide: causes and prevention. Washington, D.C.: U.S. Government Printing Office.

CHAPTER 2

PROBLEMS IN SUICIDE RESEARCH

In any research area, problems of design and interpretation must be solved before valid conclusions can be drawn. Some of these problems are general to all research, while others are unique to one topic. Problems exist because the natural world is a complex one. There are no simple "facts" which can be discovered at a glance. Information about any part of nature, and most particularly about behavior, must be obtained by the most careful observation and analysis. Otherwise, the researcher runs the risk of seeing the world in the light of his own preconceptions rather than as it really is. In this chapter, some of the specific difficulties of investigating suicide will be discussed.

METHODOLOGICAL PROBLEMS IN SUICIDE RESEARCH

DEFINING THE BEHAVIOR

It seems very obvious to point out that, in order to do research, you must know what you are working on. Yet, in behavioral research, it not infrequently appears that many workers are using a particular name but are talking about different phenomena. When they try to compare their results, they find apparent contradictions which stem from the fact that they have used the same label for different things.

Suicidologists have been aware of this problem and have worked on strict criteria to define the behaviors of suicide. Neuringer (1962) pointed out that the greatest methodological problem in suicide research concerns the definition of the behavior. (If the reader will re-read the examples at the beginning of Chapter 1, he will see why this is so.) Neuringer's paper was one of the best attempts to analyze the different possible meanings for suicide, and we will rely heavily on it in this chapter.

The most basic dimension in the definition of suicide is based on the actual behavior. Five categories of overt behavior can be noted: completed suicides, attempted suicides, suicide threats, thoughts of suicide, and no preoccupation with suicide. A possible sixth category would be that of the suicide gesture, an attempt which does not involve a real intent to die. People who make suicide gestures are like those reported by Kessel (1966) who calculate the lethal dose of a drug and then consume half of that quantity. Some investigators (for example, Dorpat and Boswell, 1963) have subdivided the attempted suicide group into gestures, ambivalent attempts, and serious (potentially lethal) attempts.

Suicidal behavior can also be analyzed in terms of lethality. The number of barbiturates taken, the height from which a jump is made, and so on allow us to calculate the chances that death would result.

The idea of lethality brings in a second basic dimension, the intent of the suicidal person. Death or continued life is not always achieved according to the person's intention. People who complete suicide may have hoped that someone would save them, while attempters may really have wanted to die and been interrupted accidentally. Psychotics and the retarded might make mistakes and not end as they planned. Thus, categorizing by intent could be more meaningful than categorizing by behavior. However, the measurement of intent is much less reliable than that of behavior. It may be possible to find out whether an attempter really meant to complete suicide, but it is hard to ascertain whether a completed suicide intended a gesture only.

Another important dimension for the definition of suicidal behavior concerns the degree of consciousness preceding the suicidal act. It has been claimed that a few individuals kill themselves in an automatized state such that they are not aware of their actions (Long, 1959). However, as we point out in Chapter 16, there is no reliable evidence that such deaths really occur. Other forms of suicide that are not consciously planned may exist, however. For example, according to Selzer and Payne (1962), people with serious suicidal preoccupation had more automobile accidents than people who were not preoccupied with suicide. It may be that the impulse toward suicide can act unconsciously and result in unplanned, "accidental" deaths.

Some suicidologists have considered long-term, gradual self-destructive behaviors as a form of suicide. Menninger (1938), for instance, used the term "chronic suicide" to refer to individuals who showed alcoholism, accident proneness, or other behaviors which are likely to result in premature death after a period of time.

Finally, we should mention that some people may be classed publicly as attempted or completed suicides even though their behavior was not motivated by self-destructive impulses. Stearns (1953) reported several cases of teenage male transvestites who hanged themselves in order to achieve orgasm, and were found dead. Clearly, the motives behind such acts must be complex, but it is probably wrong to classify them simply as suicide.

The existence of these many possible categories of suicidal behavior is important for designing and interpreting research. As long as there is some suspicion that individuals in the different categories differ from one another, the researcher must be sure that he knows in which category a particular subject belongs. Only if he is fairly sure that two categories do not differ on the factors he is concerned with can the researcher group them together. The necessity of conforming with this stricture has led to many arguments among suicidologists about the difference between attempted and completed suicides. This special problem will be discussed below.

METHODS OF INVESTIGATION

Of course, the researcher studying completed suicides cannot collect data from the dead individual. Instead, as Neuringer pointed out, he must rely on two less satisfactory methods of investigation.

(1) *The method of residuals:* The investigator can use written material and other evidence left behind, such as suicide notes, diaries, letters, previously-obtained psychological test data, and the memories of friends and relatives. This method is useful, but less than perfect. One problem is that observational distortion may occur; the friends and relatives may not remember very well what the person was like, and their memories may be colored by the fact of his suicide. The validity of the information is difficult to determine. This is true not only of reminiscences about the subject, but also about material he wrote down. If his diary recorded a tragic secret love affair, there may be no way to know whether the relationship really existed or whether it was a fantasy. Either one would be interesting in the light of the later suicide, but they are important in very different ways.

Another important problem for the method of residuals concerns the establishment of control groups. What, for example, should suicide notes be compared with? There are a number of possibilities: suicide notes written by non-suicidal subjects who pretend at the request of the researcher that they are about to kill themselves; non-suicidal letters written by suicidal people; non-suicidal letters written by non-suicidal people. None of these alternatives provides an ideal control group. Each has advantages as well as disadvantages compared to the others.

(2) *The method of substitute subjects:* The researcher can get together a group of living subjects who he feels are representative of completed suicides. Usually, the substitute subjects are those who have attempted suicide. Neuringer, like some other suicidologists, argued that suicide attempters do not resemble suicide completers, and that the method is thus invalid.

The issue is actually an empirical one, on which there is presently insufficient evidence. It should be possible to obtain an empirical answer to the question of the differences between completed and attempted suicides. At the moment, though, this important question tends to be answered on the basis of incomplete evidence. Whenever a study reveals differences between the two groups, the author tends to criticize the use of attempted suicides for research on suicide completers. When a study suggests no differences between the groups, the method of substitute subjects is defended. A representative study shows the difficulty of drawing conclusions in this area. Farberow and Shneidman (1955) compared threatened, attempted, and completed suicides and found no differences in demographic variables, socioeconomic variables, or early family environment. However, the groups differed in psychiatric diagnosis, method of attempting suicide, and previous suicidal history. Given that there are both differences and similarities between groups, how do we answer the question about the validity of substitute subjects? No definite conclusion seems to be possible.

A CONTINUUM OF SUICIDAL BEHAVIOR

It may be that all the attempts to classify different kinds of suicidal behavior are oversimplifications. Actually, all suicidal acts lie on a continuum from highly lethal to very safe. Describing certain acts as attempted or completed suicides simply emphasizes two points on the continuum. Differences between groups do not negate the existence of such a continuum. (In this country, there are no doubt significant differences on many variables between people who are very black and those who are very blond. Nonetheless, there is a continuum of skin colors.)

There is clearly a continuum of lethality. Why should there not be a broad range, rather than distinct categories, on other variables? Dorpat and Boswell (1963) noted the sex ratio (see Chapter 12) in samples of suicide gestures, ambivalent attempts, serious attempts, and completed suicides. They found that the ratio changed monotonically (without discontinuities) from the gestures to the completed suicides. This would suggest that it is valid to extrapolate, not only from attempted to completed suicides, but even from gestures to completed suicides.

SPECIAL PROBLEMS OF CONTROL

As we noted above, a proper control group for completed suicides is hard to assemble. Unfortunately, the same problem occurs when attempted suicides are the object of study. Even control of information about the suicidal group is sometimes hard to achieve. There are several factors which contribute here.

(1) *Feedback effects from the attempt.* Often, when research is done on suicide attempters, information is collected immediately after the attempt. This introduces many confounding variables. The person after his suicidal act is not necessarily similar to the way he was before it. There may be a cathartic effect from the attempt (Farberow, 1950); the individual's anger or misery may be temporarily reduced as the result of his suicidal act. The information he gives an interviewer about his feelings may not be the same as it would have been before the attempt. Therapeutic intervention, be it only stomach-pumping, may change the attempter's feelings in one direction or another. The ways in which other people have reacted to his attempt (by scorn, horror, sympathy, or whatever) may influence him. He may have brain or other tissue damage as a result of the attempt. Finally, he may try to act as "normal" as possible in order to facilitate his release from the hospital. Ideally, data from before as well as after the suicide attempt should be used, but such data are very difficult to collect, since suicide is relatively uncommon.

(2) *Effects of hospitalization.* In many situations, hospitalized suicide attempters are treated differently than other patients. They may be guarded closely and suspiciously. Their suicide while in the hospital would produce great guilt and anxiety or hostility in the staff, who stay alert in order to prevent any suicide attempts. As a result, the suicidal patient may feel guilty or rejected, even though such feelings were not present before his attempt.

(3) *Adequate control populations.* Ideally, control groups in research on suicide should be non-suicidal. In practice, totally non-suicidal

subjects are difficult to obtain. Even if people profess to be without any suicidal tendencies, the researcher must remember that there may be reluctance to confess to suicidal behavior and ideation. Most people have at one time or another at least thought about the possibility of suicide. However, it is still possible to select a control group. As we noted above, suicidal involvement is not an all-or-none matter. It is certainly possible to select a control group of people who are less seriously suicidal than the group they are being compared to. As long as one uses two groups who do not overlap on the continuum of suicidal involvement, research can proceed meaningfully.

OTHER METHODOLOGICAL PROBLEMS

When a control group is set up, the subjects in it should be matched on all relevant variables with the other comparison group. This requirement poses a real problem for suicide research. Many variables (demographic, environmental, sociological, and psychological) are consistently found to be correlated with suicidal behavior. When a researcher wants to test for the relevance of any one of the variables to suicide, he should match subjects on all the other variables in order to hold them constant. However, the range of relevant variables is so enormous that such a task is practically impossible, especially since suicide is a relatively rare behavior and subjects are scarce. Sometimes researchers match their groups for age, sex, and psychiatric disorder. The matching is rarely, if ever, more complete than that. Thus, differences which are found between suicidal and non-suicidal groups may be caused by variables other than suicidal involvement on which they are unmatched. For example, if the control group and a group of completed suicides were not matched for marital status, some factor like number of children might appear to differentiate them, since the completed suicides would be less likely to be married and, thus, less likely to have children.

The particular subject population that is chosen may bring bias to the results. Siewers and Davidoff (1943) compared two groups of attempted suicides: those admitted to a general hospital and those in a psychiatric hospital. The two groups differed on many variables. Those in the general hospital were younger and less disturbed than those in the psychiatric hospital. They also differed in occupation, religious affiliation, method of suicide used, and the presence of organic disease.

Not only are different groups of suicides unlike each other on important variables, but samples of suicides may not be representative of the total suicidal population. When Shneidman and Farberow (1961) traced 5,906 attempted suicides in Los Angeles County, they could find sufficient data on only 2,652. Research in other areas has shown that the untraced persons may differ significantly from those who are traced (Lester, 1969). The same objection applies to studies of suicide notes. Shneidman and Farberow reported that thirty-six percent of completed and one percent of attempted suicides left notes that were found. To what extent are the note writers typical of suicidal people in general?

Finally, we should discuss the problem of level of statistical significance for research on suicide. (The preface defines this term.) It has been difficult to find many significant differences between suicidal and nonsuicidal subjects. Neuringer and Kolstoe (1966) suggested that a less stringent level than five percent should be accepted for suicide research, since many important relationships might otherwise be missed. However, changing the required significance level would mean that many unreliable and false relationships would be accepted. It is hard enough for results to be replicated at the present maximum probability levels. We could make a case for demanding *more* stringent significance levels so that the results of suicide research would be reliable. If no reliable results were then to be found, it would be clear that thinking about the causes of suicide requires a drastic reconceptualization rather than just a change in significance levels.

CONCLUSION

Research on suicide almost always involves correlational rather than experimental methods. For this reason, it may be difficult to conclude accurately in which direction causality is operating (e.g., does being thin cause suicidal tendencies, or does being suicidal cause people to lose their appetites?). Sampling and establishing control groups are also problems in suicide research, since suicidal behavior is relatively rare. Defining suicide and deciding whether attempters and completers are to be considered as different groups add to the difficulty of research on suicide. Biased results may be found when research is done on a particular sample that is not typical of all suicidal people.

BIBLIOGRAPHY

DORPAT, T. L., and BOSWELL, J. W. 1963. An evaluation of suicidal intent in suicide attempts. *Comp. Psychiat.* 4: 117–25.

FARBEROW, N. L. 1950. Personality patterns of suicidal mental hospital patients. *Genet. Psychol. Monog.* 42, no. 1: 3–79.

FARBEROW, N. L., and SHNEIDMAN, E. S. 1955. Attempted, threatened, and completed suicide. *J. Abnorm. Soc. Psychol.* 50: 230.

KESSEL, N. 1966. The respectability of self-poisoning and the fashion of survival. *J. Psychosom. Res.* 10: 29–36.

LESTER, D. 1969. The subject as a source of bias in psychological research. *J. Gen. Psychol.* 81: 237–48.

LONG, R. H. 1959. Barbiturates, automatization, and suicide. *Insurance Counseling J.* April: 299–307.

MENNINGER, K. 1938. *Man against himself.* New York: Harcourt Brace Jovanovich, Inc.

NEURINGER, C., and KOLSTOE, R. H. 1966. Suicide research and the non-rejection of the null hypothesis. *Percept. Mot. Skills.* 22: 115–18.

NEURINGER, C. 1962. Methodological problems in suicide research. *J. Consult. Psychol.* 26: 273–78.

SELZER, M. L., and PAYNE, C. E. 1962. Automobile accidents, suicide, and unconscious motivation. *Amer. J. Psychiat.* 119: 237–40.

SHNEIDMAN, E. S., and FARBEROW, N. L. 1961. Statistical comparisons between committed and attempted suicides. In N. L. Farberow and E. S. Shneidman, eds. *The cry for help.* New York: McGraw-Hill Book Company, pp. 19–47.

SIEWERS, A. B., and DAVIDOFF, E. 1943. Attempted suicide. *Psychiat. Quart.* 17: 520–34.

STEARNS, A. W. 1953. Cases of probable suicide in young persons without obvious motivation. *J. Maine Med. Assoc.* 44: 16–23.

CHAPTER 3

LABELLING DEATH: TAXONOMIES OF DYING

Our language leads us to consider life and death as opposites, states which can be present only one at a time. Many people over the centuries have assumed that there is some definite moment when the transition from life to death occurs. Earlier in history, there were even attempts to find the moment of transition and to weigh the soul by keeping the dying person on a set of scales. It was expected that the person's weight would decrease slightly as the soul departed from the body.

Advances in medical and surgical skills have made it clear that there is no precise moment when a person passes from being alive to being dead. Absence of breathing or of heartbeat does not always mean that the process of death has become irreversible. Rather than looking for the moment when life vanishes, physicians now try to determine when the gradual process can no longer be reversed. This determination, of course, involves detection of clinical signs, the pattern of which indicates the extent of the patient's progression toward death.[1]

THE PSYCHOLOGICAL MOMENT OF DEATH

When the goal is to cure physical illness, bodily signs of death are objective evidence that can be used. In the study of suicide, an equally

[1] The Harvard *Lampoon* recently published a Test of Clinical Death, which included such signs as "X's where the eyes should be," "a lot of talk about the Happy Hunting Grounds," and "a funny smell on the ward."

important consideration is the subjective judgment of the conditions under which a person is considered dead. The question is an interesting one in itself, since (as the reader will see) people do not agree very well on the topic. It is also of importance for the study of suicide, since self-destruction could be made more likely if a person was considered somehow dead even while he was still living and conscious.

In one study of the subjective time of death (Kalish, 1965), college students were asked to choose one of seven alternatives as the circumstances under which a person is considered to be dead. The seven choices were: a) when he first learns he is going to die; b) when he first enters a hospital, knowing that he will never leave alive; c) when he first enters a nursing home knowing that he will never leave alive; d) when he loses self-awareness; e) when he becomes very senile; f) when he wants to die or gives up on life; g) when his heart stops beating.

Only half of the students used the biological criterion of cessation of heartbeats as the event that signified death. The others used psychological criteria instead. Thirty-five percent said the person was dead when he lost self-awareness, and thirty-five percent said wanting to die or giving up on life indicated death (some students checked more than one alternative, so the figures total more than one hundred percent).

There seem to be four basic ways of defining death (Kalish, 1966):

Physical death:
a) biological death, when the organs stop functioning.
b) clinical death, when the organism no longer functions but the organs continue to live. If a person fatally injured in an accident is kept alive mechanically until his heart can be transplanted, he is clinically dead for some time before his biological death.

Psychological death: the individual ceases to be aware of his own existence. He does not know who he is or even that he is. This can occur, of course, well before physical death, if the person is comatose for a long period.

Social death:
a) self-perceived: the individual accepts the notion that he is, for all practical purposes, dead. An example of this would occur in the case of voodoo death (Cannon, 1957). The person believes that a spell or curse has been placed on him and that he will die within some brief period. He stops functioning, refuses nourishment, and waits for death to occur—which it often does.
b) other-perceived: people who know the individual act as if he is dead or nonexistent. An elderly relative is placed in a nursing home and forgotten. In ancient times, a leper was cast out of society and expected never to have social contact with healthy people.

Anthropological death: the individual is cut off from a particular community and spoken of as if he is dead. An Orthodox Jewish family, for example, may mourn for a child who marries a Gentile as if he had physically died. (When he dies biologically, however, they may mourn again, thus showing that they discriminate between anthropological and physical death).

CLASSIFYING DEATH STATES

The established medical scheme for classifying states of death stresses the causes (like illness) and the *modes* of death. Four modes are commonly recognized: accidental death, homicide, suicide, and natural death. This classification is adequate for its original purpose—the ascription of responsibility for death to the right person or cause. However, it does not allow fine enough distinctions for use when a person has been motivated to seek his own death. For example, a person may provoke an assailant to murder him. The death is clearly to be classified as a homicide, but this categorization does not take into account the dead person's suicidal motivation.

E. S. Shneidman (1963) has proposed a more complete classification which allows more meaningful description of a death. First, the system involves a new classification of the behaviors associated with death:

a) *cessation* is defined as the stopping of any (further) conscious experience. It is the demise of psychic processes.

b) *termination* is the end of the body's physiological functioning. In the Christian view of an afterlife, termination can occur without cessation.

c) *interruption* is the temporary stopping of conscious awareness, as in coma.

d) *continuation* is the ongoing conscious experience of events.

These four terms define physical death as it is experienced by the dying person and by those caring for him. A second variable in Shneidman's classification involves the role of the person in his own death. Four basic roles were proposed:

a) *intentioned* (or premeditated). The person plays a direct and conscious role in his own demise. Many, but not all, suicidal deaths would be labeled "intentioned," as would some homicidal deaths, like the victim-premeditated homicides mentioned above (Wolfgang, 1959). Some deaths which are considered accidental might be intentioned, as when a person teases an animal until it kills him. A natural death could sometimes be intentioned too, if a person deliberately exposed himself to disease. Clearly, all intentioned deaths are suicidal, but their suicidal aspects may not be noted by those who certify the mode of death. Some deaths may occur because of a person's own deliberate actions and yet not be intentioned.

b) *subintentioned* (or submeditated). The individual plays an indirect, covert, or unconscious role in his demise, as when a person fails to act for his own best welfare. Some suicidal deaths could be subintentioned; for example, a diabetic might go on a drinking binge, knowing that alcohol is very bad for him.

c) *unintentioned* (or unmeditated). The person plays no significant role in his own demise.

d) *contraintentioned*. The person acts the role of someone about to cease (in Shneidman's terminology), but he intends not to do so. The individual who threatens suicide, but has no intention of hurting himself, is playing a contraintentioned role.

Shneidman's classification has not come into broad use. For that reason, we will use the ordinary terminology in the rest of this book. However, the reader will benefit from understanding the kind of analysis of death implied in Shneidman's taxonomy before he reads more about suicidal behavior.

CLASSIFICATION OF SUICIDAL BEHAVIOR

Generally, suicidal acts have been classified in terms of the outcome. If the person injured himself deliberately but did not die, he was said to have *attempted* suicide. If he died as a result of his act, he was said to have *committed* suicide. We shall use the term attempted suicide, but for those who die, we prefer a term that is becoming more widely used: *completed* suicide. The idea that a person can complete suicide stresses that suicidal behaviors are ranged on a continuum from mildly lethal to completely lethal.

The classification into suicide attempters and completers is convenient, but it may obscure facts about the motivation of the suicidal behavior. As pointed out in Chapter 1, a person may fully intend to die, but be rescued. Another person may only want to make a dramatic gesture, but may die because of unforeseen circumstances.

If the nature of suicidal behavior is obscured by use of the attempted vs. completed dichotomy, why is it still used? One reason is a long-standing belief among suicidologists that those who attempt and those who complete suicide are very different kinds of people. For example, as we will discuss in Chapter 12, suicide is completed preponderantly by males and attempted preponderantly by females. However, there is little information available to help us conclude that the populations of attempters and completers really are (or really are not) different. Nonetheless, to allow for the possibility that the groups vary in quality rather than simply severity of suicidal impulses, we will not group attempters and completers together when discussing suicide research.

DEATH BY ACCIDENT

According to Shneidman's classification, a person may bring about his own death because of some wish of which he is not fully aware ("subintentioned"). This raises the question whether people who die from car accidents resemble those whose death is intentioned and brought about by other means. (It may even be the case, of course, that an automobile can be used as a means of premeditated suicide.)

It appears that a history of driving accidents and a history of suicidal preoccupation may often go together (Selzer and Payne, 1962; Selzer et al., 1968). In one study, suicidal psychiatric patients had about twice as many accidents as non-suicidal patients. In another study, a group of drivers involved in fatal accidents more frequently had histories of suicide attempts or thoughts than a group of average drivers.

Psychological tests seem to indicate, however, that suicidal people differ in a number of ways from most careless drivers (Preston, 1964). Another study on the same topic (Paffenbarger, et al., 1969) concluded that anxiety and despair characterize the person who will commit suicide, while irresponsibility and nonchalance are characteristic of the person who will die in an accident.

OTHER SELF-DESTRUCTIVE BEHAVIORS

Many forms of behavior are not immediately lethal but lead, in the long run, to self-injury or death. Some writers (like Menninger, 1938) have considered these behaviors to be closely related to suicide. Alcoholism, drug addiction, polysurgery (the practice of having multiple operations for no real medical reason), and so on may all be considered as subintentioned suicidal behavior. Some of them are quite effective as "interruption," since they yield temporary unconsciousness. Mild self-injurious behaviors may also be related to suicide—for example, nail-biting, and hair-pulling. Menninger was willing to accept all of these behaviors as qualitatively similar to suicide. Since no real research on this question has been done, it remains a matter of opinion.

OFFICIAL STATISTICS ON SUICIDE

When a coroner decides whether a death is a suicide, or when a county health board issues statistics about the suicide rate in its area, such fine points as whether nail-biting resembles suicide are not considered. In fact, one may wonder exactly what they do consider. One suicidologist, Douglas (1967), has severely criticized the accuracy of certification of suicidal deaths. As Douglas pointed out, the meaning of the term "suicide" may vary tremendously over time, among geographical regions, and among different religious groups. One coroner in the United States has been reported as certifying deaths as suicides only if a suicide note was found with the body. Since estimates of the proportion of suicides leaving notes range from ten to forty percent, it seems likely that this particular coroner was grossly underestimating the number of suicides in his area.

Not only may there be a systematic bias about the certification of deaths by suicide, there may be actual attempts to conceal suicidal deaths. There are clearly many reasons to attempt concealment. Some religious groups refuse normal funeral rites to the suicide. Insurance policies often do not pay the survivors any benefits after a death by suicide, and they frequently pay more for a death judged accidental than for a suicide or a natural death. We can only presume that the reporting of suicidal deaths would be more accurate if less opprobrium were attached to suicide by society.

Until better criteria for deciding when a suicide has occurred are available, coroners can hardly be expected to use consistent decision methods. Each coroner is now essentially left to himself to determine whether particular tests should be made (e.g., for the presence of barbiturates in the body). Coroners also set their own standards for inferring whether the dead person was motivated toward suicide. These standards are personally and culturally determined; for example, a woman who was known to have been disappointed in love might be certified as a suicide when a man would not.

Some attempts are being made to find good criteria for deciding when a person was motivated toward suicide. At the Los Angeles Suicide Prevention Center, psychologists and psychiatrists regularly participate in "psychological autopsies." In these investigations, the writing of a suicide note and other pre-death activities are studied. The family, friends, and physician of the dead person are interviewed, and an attempt is made to develop an accurate picture of the last days of the person's life. However, since the psychological autopsy requires hours of work by many trained people, it is doubtful that most coroners will start to use this method in the foreseeable future.

CONCLUSION

Death is a gradual process, and no one moment can be identified as the time when it occurs. From the viewpoint of suicidology, the question of when physical death occurs is less important than the individual's subjective experience of death. He may consider himself "as good as dead" when his body is still functioning, or he may expect his consciousness and awareness to continue beyond bodily death. Another important question involves the role the person plays in his own death. He may help bring it about without being conscious of what he is doing. Official certifications of death do not usually attend to any of these subtle questions and they probably underestimate the actual incidence of suicide.

BIBLIOGRAPHY

CANNON, W. B. 1957. Voodoo death. *Psychosom. Med.* 19: 182–90.

DOUGLAS, J. D. 1967. *The social meanings of suicide.* Princeton: Princeton University Press.

KALISH, R. A. 1965. A continuum of subjectively perceived death. Paper given at meeting of Gerontological Society, Los Angeles.

MENNINGER, K. 1938. *Man against himself.* New York: Harcourt Brace Jovanovich, Inc.

PAFFENBARGER, R. S., KING, S. H., and WING, A. L. 1969. Chronic disease in former college students: IX. Characteristics that predispose to suicide and accidental death. *Amer. J. Pub. Hlth.,* 59: 900–908.

PRESTON, C. E. 1964. Accident proneness in attempted suicide and in automobile victims. *J. Consult. Psychol.* 28: 79–82.

SELZER, M. L., and PAYNE, C. E., 1962. Automobile accidents, suicide, and unconscious motivation. *Amer. J. Psychiat.* 119: 237–40.

SELZER, M. L., ROGERS, J. E., and KERN, S. 1968. Fatal accidents. *Amer. J. Psychiat.* 124: 1028–36.

SHNEIDMAN, E. S. 1963. Orientations toward death. In R. White, ed. *The study of lives.* New York: Atherton, pp. 200–27.

WOLFGANG, M. E. 1959. Suicide by means of victim-precipitated homicide. *J. Clin. Exp. Psychopathol.* 20: 335–49.

CHAPTER 4

HEREDITY AND ENVIRONMENT IN THE CAUSATION OF SUICIDE

When more than one person in a family has killed himself, gossips may begin to whisper about some hereditary taint which they expect to result in more suicides. The possibility of inheritance of suicide may create anxiety in the living members of the family. Even a child who cannot remember his father's suicide may wonder whether the same death is in store for him, with or without his volition.

Is there a real basis for these people's suspicions and fears? Can suicide be passed along genetically, as eye color or hemophilia are inherited? Or, alternatively, is suicide purely the result of an individual's experiences? This chapter will attempt to answer these questions as well as research evidence allows.

GENETIC FACTORS

The question of heredity versus environment is always difficult to answer, of course, since no one can live without an environment. If the results of genetic factors do not show until late in life, they can never show in their pure form, since the influence of environment has been going on for so long. There is evidence that even the environment of the uterus in the period between conception and birth can influence behavior. Nevertheless, some attempts have been made to try to trace genetic factors in suicide.

Some years ago, a common approach to this problem was to study family trees. This method does not differentiate hereditary from environmental influences, since no two people ever experience exactly the same family environment. (In a family of four children, for example, the eldest may experience an environment containing two young brothers and a very young sister, while the youngest may experience two older brothers and a very superior elder sister.) Nevertheless, the study of genealogical tables demonstrates that some families have a very high incidence of suicide, which confirms the belief that suicide does not "strike" at random. Figure 1 shows an example of a family with much

A FAMILY WITH MANY SUICIDAL MEMBERS
(from Shapiro, 1935)

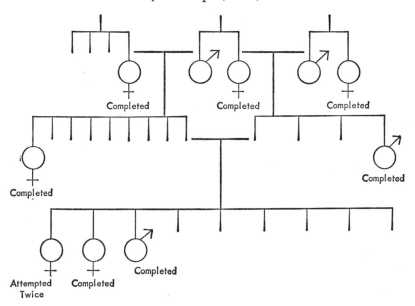

suicidal behavior. Such examples, however, do not provide real evidence for genetic determination of suicide.

A more appropriate way to study genetic factors in suicide involves research with twins. Monozygotic twins, who develop from a single ovum, are genetically identical. Dizygotic twins, who start their development as separate ova, are no more similar genetically than non-twin siblings. Kallman (1953) studied eighteen pairs of identical twins and twenty-one pairs of fraternal twins among whom at least one of the twins had killed himself. If suicide were genetically caused, we would

identical twin pairs to have concordant behavior; that is, if
were a suicide, his co-twin would also exhibit suicidal be-
among fraternal twin pairs, concordance would be no higher
ing ordinary siblings. Kallman did not find any differences between concordance of suicide in monozygotic and in dizygotic twin pairs.

When Lester (1968) re-analyzed Kallman's data, using more appropriate statistical methods, it appeared that there were significantly more
concordant suicides among the monozygotic twins, as would be the case
if a genetic factor were involved. However, since Kallman's twin pairs
were not a random sample, we cannot conclude that a hereditary effect
is definitely present.

It is impossible to draw a definite conclusion about the importance
of genetic factors. Identical twins may be treated very differently from
fraternal twins, and an interaction between this environmental effect and
the genetic factors could obscure the latter. But it is possible to say that
no clear demonstration of the inheritance of suicide has ever occurred.

CONSTITUTIONAL FACTORS

To some extent, a person's physical constitution is influenced by genetic
factors and to some extent it is determined by his environment (for
example, diet available during childhood). Many investigators have
examined physiological differences between suicidal and non-suicidal
subjects. Although strictly genetic factors do not seem to be operative in
suicide, perhaps the combination of certain hereditary and environmental effects is instrumental in leading to suicide. Investigation of this problem has stressed several main areas: physical state (illness vs. good
health), physique, and physiological (biochemical) state.

PHYSICAL STATE

Illness can produce stress that may contribute to the development of
suicidal behavior. A number of studies have found that the physical
health of suicides a few months before their death was worse than that
of a non-suicidal group. In one study (Dorpat et al., 1968), seventy
percent of the completed suicides appeared to have had an acute illness at
the time of death. The illness seemed to have contributed to suicide by
affecting the people's moods. Depressive reactions were produced by fear
of death, pain, illness, and surgery, and through the social isolation that
accompanies illness.

It must be noted that some researchers have found *no* relation between suicidal behavior and physical illness in their studies. No one, however, has reported a negative relationship (i.e., an association of suicide with good health and non-suicide with poor health). Poor health can probably contribute to suicidal behavior, but it is one of the less important factors in actually causing suicide.

PHYSIQUE

A relationship between physique and personality exists in many people's implicit personality theories; we have "the jolly fat man" and the dangerous man with "a lean and hungry look." Some years ago Sheldon (1942) proposed that human beings could be assigned to one of three predominant body types, each of which was associated with particular personality traits. Fat people with highly developed viscera were given the name "endomorphs" and were thought to be sociable and pleasure-loving. "Mesomorphs" were heavily muscled, and rather brash and insensitive. "Ectomorphs" were thin and had little muscular development; they were shy, intellectual, and hypersensitive to all kinds of stimulation. Sheldon felt that endomorphs had a strong aversion to death and that suicide was rare among them. Ectomorphs, on the other hand, with their shyness and hypersensitivity, were thought to have frequent suicidal tendencies.

No one, including Sheldon, has made an empirical test of this supposition. Some studies have examined the relationship between weight and suicide, however. In general, it seems that underweight or overweight people are more likely to kill themselves than people of normal weight—although one study (Robinson, 1962) revealed that men who were *slightly* overweight actually had a lower suicide rate than men of normal weight.

We must remember, when thinking about physique and suicide, that causality need not work only in one direction. People who become suicidal may have changes in physique due to their mood. They may change their dietary habits and become overweight or underweight because of their obsession with suicide.

PHYSIOLOGICAL STATE

The research that has been done on biochemical changes and suicide is far too complex to be dealt with here. The bodies of suicides do seem to differ in several ways from those of people who have died accidentally. The former show changes that are associated with long-term stress. There is, however, no evidence that biochemical changes lead to suicide;

the changes are probably the result of the same stresses which brought about the suicide.

THE EFFECTS OF ENVIRONMENT

Genetic factors in suicide and the combined effect of heredity and environment as they are reflected in an individual's physical constitution have been examined. The effect of environment—the possibility that learning and experience in the course of life determine suicidal behavior —will be discussed next. Our major emphasis here will be on comparisons of suicidal behavior in different cultural groups. The problem of individual experiences and their influence, which is relevant here, will be discussed at length in the next chapter.

In the study of suicide, it has become clear that there are considerable differences in incidence of the behavior from one culture to another. In most cases, quite a lot is known about the culture under consideration: its child-rearing practices, its values, its social organization. Cross-cultural comparisons have thus presented a very valuable means of testing hypotheses about the causes of suicidal behavior.

Suicide occurs, of course, in primitive, non-literate societies as well as in modern ones. Ethnographers have collected a considerable amount of information on suicidal behavior in primitive societies. This discussion, however, will be limited to investigation of cross-comparisons between well-documented modern social groups. This limitation will be imposed, despite the fact that primitive suicidal behavior is often very interesting, because it appears that information collected by early ethnographers was not especially reliable. R. Naroll (1962) has analyzed the reports of early ethnographers in an attempt to find sources of bias, and he has concluded that estimates of suicidal behavior are biased by the inaccuracy of the informant, by the ethnographer himself, and by the anthropologist who interprets the ethnographer's data. When modern developed societies are studied, it is possible to obtain data from so many sources that possible biases can cancel each other out. It is also possible to go back and remeasure suspicious data, which obviously can not be done for a culture existing only in the ethnographer's subjective report.

CULTURAL DIFFERENCES IN REACTING
TO CRISES

Since suicidal behavior appears to occur most often in a crisis situation, it is worthwhile to note that reactions to crisis are strongly determined by culture. One culture may condone highly emotional reactions and even criticize a person who remains calm, while another may insist on complete stoicism in the face of crisis. Trautman (1961) noted that Puerto Rican women in a crisis situation may respond by the hysterical *ataque nervioso,* in which the individual withdraws from the problem by falling to the ground in a stupor. Other research (McCandless, 1968) has looked at the differences between people of Indian and of African origin living in Guyana. The Indians have little in the way of culturally sanctioned behavior for crises of rage; they are simply supposed to be obedient and to inhibit their reaction to others no matter what the crisis. The Africans, on the other hand, have many culturally approved ways of expressing themselves during a crisis. (It is notable that the African population has a very low suicide rate, while that of the Indians is high.) Another elaborate way of responding to a crisis is seen in the Malay *amok,* which differs dramatically from most culturally approved Western responses to crisis situations. The person who runs *amok* essentially does everything he has been told not to do. He is highly destructive to property and to people who get in his way. Above all, however, he "tempts fate" by calling out special words which are forbidden by taboo—for example, the magic name for tigers which is thought to attract them to the scene. If the words really had the power attributed to them by the culture, his behavior would be suicidal in effect.

The reader may notice that, although the *amok* is very different from any crisis response presently approved by Western cultures, it is somewhat similar to such behaviors as heavy and belligerent drinking or reckless driving during a crisis. Looking at the historical background of modern Western societies, too, we find that the Vikings had a culturally sanctioned state known as being "berserk," in which a warrior hurled himself into combat with animals or other men without thought for his own safety. Fortunately for the "berserker," other warriors were frightened by this behavior and tended to flee rather than taking advantage of the "berserker's" poorly guarded approach.

CULTURAL DIFFERENCES IN SUICIDAL BEHAVIOR

A great deal of research has involved differences in suicide among different cultures. The differences in suicidal behavior of the many cultural groups living in Hawaii have been studied by Richard Kalish (1968). The ratio of completed suicides to suicide attempts ranged from 5:100 for the Puerto Ricans to 73:100 for the Chinese. There is a high percentage of young Hawaiian, Filipino, and Puerto Rican people who complete suicide, while there are more older people who complete suicide among the Koreans, Japanese, and Chinese.

Suicidal behavior in Japan has been found to differ considerably from that in the United States (Iga, 1961). Of people completing suicide, a far larger proportion are women in Japan than in the United States. The Japanese suicide rate is higher in rural than in urban areas, which is also the opposite of the American pattern. Rather than having the highest suicide rate occur in one age group, as is the case in the U.S., the Japanese have two age groups that show peaks of suicidal behavior. Iga attributed these differences in suicidal behavior to a weakness in personality development, a strong sense of shame after failure, and a more favorable attitude toward suicide in the Japanese. There seems to be no real evidence for any differences between Americans and Japanese in terms of maturity of personality. However, suicide has long been socially approved in Japan as a solution to certain problems. The ceremony of *harakiri* was considered a very appropriate way for a respectable person to negate some humiliation which had come upon him. Perhaps this ancient approval of suicide under the right conditions accounts for the higher rural suicide rate in Japan, since the old traditions are more likely to persist in rural areas.

SUICIDE IN SCANDINAVIA

Many suicidologists have investigated and tried to explain the peculiar phenomenon of differing suicide rates in Scandinavia. In Denmark and Sweden, the completed suicide rate is about 17 per 100,000, while in Norway it is only about 7 per 100,000 per year.

One hypothesis about this difference, frequently voiced by political conservatives, is that the establishment of a welfare state leads to a high suicide rate. A welfare system supposedly leads to boredom, impairment of incentive to work, diminished zest for living, and a lack of frustration tolerance, and thus to suicide. Farber (1965) has tried to determine whether the establishment of a welfare state actually did affect the differences in suicide rate. It appears that the differences in suicide rate in Norway and Denmark exist in spite of the fact that both have welfare systems. When the welfare system was instituted in Denmark, the suicide rate actually showed a moderate decline, especially among the older people who benefited most from the welfare system. Farber also noted that Saskatchewan has the most highly developed welfare system in Canada, but that its suicide rate is lower than that of the surrounding provinces; similarly, the suicide rate in the United States fell after the social legislations of the New Deal were introduced.

A major attempt to explain the differences among the suicide rates of Norway, Denmark, and Sweden has been made by Hendin, who made a psychoanalytic study of the three countries. He interviewed attempted suicides, non-suicidal patients, and nurses in order to get an understanding of the culture of each country. The interviews were supplemented with studies of folklore, literature, drama, and cartoons. Based on the information gathered from each country, Hendin developed a brief description of the motivation for suicide in each of the three Scandinavian countries.

In Sweden, according to Hendin, there is

> a "performance" type of suicide. Based on rigid performance expectations with strong self-hatred for failure and set in the matrix of a particular Swedish affectivity problem, such performance suicide is also traceable to an early mother-child separation. (Hendin, 1965, p. 146)

In Denmark, on the other hand, there appears

> primarily a "dependency-loss" kind of suicide. Specific Danish features are a tendency toward passivity, oversensitivity to abandonment, and an effective use of the technique of arousing guilt in others; once again, these features have their basis in Danish family patterns. (Hendin, 1965, p. 146)

Norway derives from its rural areas

> what is best described as a "moral" form of suicide. It stems from aggressive antisocial behavior and strong guilt feelings aroused by such behavior, with the entire constellation cast in a puritanical setting. (Hendin, 1965, p. 147)

Hendin considered the differences in suicide in the three countries to stem from differences in child-rearing practices.

With respect to the high Swedish suicide rate, Hendin says,

> The child's early separation from the mother stimulates anger and at the same time deflates self-esteem. The control over anger and other strong emotions requires that anger be handled with a good deal of detachment. Few combinations provide such fertile soil for suicide as affective deadening combined with, and based on, the need to control aggression. . . . Because of rigid expectations for his own performance . . . the male becomes vulnerable to self-hatred and suicide if he fails. . . .

A similar kind of explanation is given for the Danes.

> What is apparently basic to the Danish vulnerability to depression and suicide is the unique forms of dependence seen in Denmark. . . . The Danish child's dependence on his mother is encouraged far more than

that of the American child . . . the child's aggressiveness is strictly checked. . . . With an openness that was both appealing and yet almost childlike in manner, (adult) male and female patients spoke of having been too egocentric to care deeply for anyone else. . . . Several patients said that they only took something from people without giving anything back.

As for the Norwegians,

As a rule, Norwegian and Danish mothers differ significantly in expressing the mother-child tie. The Norwegian child is given much physical freedom to play and run around . . . (The mother) will try to derive happiness from the child's independent accomplishments and live vicariously through them. . . . In Norway patients made little effort in the tones of their voice or in their words, movements and facial expressions to disguise their anger.

Other researchers (Block and Christiansen, 1966) tried to test Hendin's hypotheses about maternal attitudes by studying the beliefs of students in Denmark, Sweden, and Norway. Their study supported Hendin's ideas best for Norway and Denmark and least for Sweden. Evidence was found to support Hendin's concepts of the importance of competition, maternal authority, physical freedom and autonomy, and the use of teasing in child-rearing, but not to support the ideas of dependency, toleration for aggressiveness, and tolerance for affect.

Farber (1968) has also attempted to explain the difference between the Danish and Norwegian suicide rates. He looked at both sociological and psychological variables, and came to these conclusions:

1) Danes view life less hopefully than do Norwegians.
2) Danes express a weaker sense of competence than Norwegians.
3) Danes express aggression less easily than Norwegians.
4) Danish neighbors are seen as less succorant than Norwegians.
5) The Danes are more tolerant of suicide than Norwegians.

It is clear that these five conditions could lead to a higher Danish than Norwegian suicide rate.

CONCLUSION

As far as it is possible to tell, genetic factors are not responsible for suicide. Some constitutional factors, such as ill health, may predispose a person to suicide, while environmental effects, especially those due to cultural factors in child-rearing practices, seem to produce considerable differences in suicidal behavior. When specific cultural practices are examined, it is possible to develop logical explanations for these differences. However, the question is still unanswered whether it is a particular personality pattern in some individuals, produced within the culture, that leads to suicide, or whether the culture could push any personality toward suicide under the right conditions.

BIBLIOGRAPHY

BLOCK, J., and CHRISTIANSEN, B. 1966. A test of Hendin's hypothesis relating suicide in Scandinavia to child-rearing orientations. *Scand. J. Psychol.* 7: 267–68.

BUNNEY, W. F., and FAWCETT, J. A. 1965. Possibility of a biochemical test for suicidal potential. *Arch. Gen. Psychiat.* 13: 232–39.

DORPAT, T. L., ANDERSON, W. F., and RIPLEY, H. S. 1968. The relationship of physical illness to suicide. In H. RESNIK, ed., *Suicidal Behaviors,* Boston: Little, Brown and Company, pp. 209–19.

DUBLIN, L., and BUNZEL, B. 1933. *To be or not to be.* New York: Harrison Smith and Robert Haas.

FARBER, M. L. 1965. Suicide and the welfare state. *Ment. Hyg.* 49: 371–73.

HENDIN, H. 1965. *Suicide and Scandinavia.* New York: Doubleday & Company, Inc.

IGA, M. 1961. Cultural factors in suicide of Japanese youth with focus on personality. *Sociol. Social Res.* 46: 75–90.

KALISH, R. A. 1968. Suicide. *Bull. Suicidol.* December: 37–43.

KALLMAN, F. J. 1953. *Heredity in health and mental disease.* New York: W. W. Norton & Company, Inc.

KALLMAN, F. J., DePORTE, J., DePORTE, E., and FEINGOLD, L. 1949. Suicide in twins and only children. *Amer. J. Hum. Genet.* 1: 113–26.

LESTER, D. 1968. Note on the inheritance of suicide. *Psychol. Rep.* 22: 320.

McCANDLESS, F. D. 1968. Suicide and the communication of rage. *Amer. J. Psychiat.* 125: 197–205.

NAROLL, R. 1962. *Data quality control.* Glencoe, Ill.: The Free Press.

ROBINSON, P. I. 1962. Suicide. *Postgrad. Med.* 32: 154–59.

SHAPIRO, L. B. 1935. Suicide. *J. Nerv. Ment. Dis.* 81: 547–53.

SHELDON, W. H. 1942. *The varieties of temperament.* New York: Harper & Row, Publishers.

TRAUTMAN, E. C. 1961. Suicide attempts of Puerto Rican immigrants. *Psychiat. Quart.* 35: 544–54.

TUCKMAN, J., YOUNGMAN, W. F., and KRIEZMAN, G. 1966. Suicide and physical illness. *J. Gen. Psychol.* 75: 291–95.

CHAPTER 5

CHILDHOOD EXPERIENCES AND SUBSEQUENT SUICIDE

It is a truism that unhappy and disorganized childhoods lead to unhappy and disorganized lives. Tolstoy tells us that happy families are all alike and unhappy ones are all unhappy in their own ways. We may ask whether particular kinds of unhappy childhoods lead to particular kinds of unhappy lives. A child's life may be disturbed in many different ways: through the parents' marital disharmony, loss of a parent, severe punishment, and so on. In this chapter, the relationship between particular kinds of childhood disturbances and the tendency of the adult to be suicidal will be discussed.

FAMILY DISORGANIZATION

One way to tell whether a family is in trouble is to see whether its members are using the services of community resources such as courts or health and welfare agencies. The more difficulty a family is having, the more likely its members are to end up in court (whether for crimes or for divorce proceedings), or to use public welfare agencies rather than managing their lives on their own. Some research indicates that suicidal people (especially attempted suicides) come from families who have had to use community resources to deal with their problems. Unfortunately, it is not clear to what extent non-suicidal persons have had similar family troubles. There is, however, a general feeling among suicide researchers that the suicidal adult has experienced as a child an unusual amount of economic deprivation, neglect, and marital disharmony.

PUNISHMENT EXPERIENCES

Elsewhere in this book we will discuss the concept of inward and outward direction of aggression—the idea that resentment and rage may be expressed by an individual in a characteristic way by either attacks on himself or on other people. This idea has been used in the study of suicide by the sociologists Henry and Short (1954). These authors have suggested that the tendency to turn aggression inward or outward is learned in the course of experience of punishment during childhood. They felt that the child who is given love-oriented or psychological punishment ("Mommy won't love you if you do that.") learns to inhibit his aggression, since aggressiveness toward the parent leads to withdrawal of love. The aggressiveness of the psychologically punished child is then turned inward. The child who is punished physically, on the other hand, is not threatened with loss of love when he attacks the parent, and he learns to express his aggression outwardly.

Some researchers have tried to test Henry and Short's ideas against empirical evidence. M. Gold (1958) suggested that certain groups are more likely to have experienced physical punishment as children than others—males more than females, enlisted army men more than officers, rural dwellers more than urban dwellers, and blacks more than whites. If Henry and Short's theory is correct, then, the first member of each of those pairs should show a suicide rate which was relatively low as compared to their homicide rate. Gold's findings agreed with the prediction. However, it may be that Gold's broad categories concealed some factor that was really responsible for the difference (perhaps status or educational level).

Two studies (Lester, 1966, 1967) did not support Henry and Short's prediction. First, no correlation appeared to exist between discipline techniques and suicide and homicide rates in nonliterate societies. (However, the reader should consider the criticisms of the available information on non-literate societies that are detailed in the last chapter.) Students' memories of childhood discipline and their later suicidal tendencies were also investigated. Again, there seemed to be no relation between suicidal behavior and discipline experiences.

Perhaps a clear relationship will some day be shown between suicidal behavior and childhood punishment experiences, but even if that should occur, there still will be questions about a cause-and-effect relationship. The conclusion that punishment experiences determine suicidal behavior could not be assumed. Instead, as R. Q. Bell has pointed out, children with particular behavioral tendencies may elicit from their parents certain kinds of punishment. A child who responds well to verbal scolding may never be spanked, while another child in the same family may be harder to control and may make the parents feel they have no alternative but physical punishment.

LEONARD'S DEVELOPMENTAL THEORY

Calista Leonard (1967) has proposed an interesting developmental theory of suicide that has not yet been empirically tested. She suggested that the second and third years of life were crucial for the development of suicidal tendencies. During those years, the child begins his struggle for independence and autonomy from the mother. His own identity begins to develop. These are difficult tasks for the child, and they are made even harder because he is still dependent on the mother. Thus, the second and third years involve tremendous conflict between the growing need for autonomy and the fear of alienating the mother while she is still needed.

Leonard felt that the conflict between independence and dependence can be resolved in three ways, each of which is somewhat associated with a kind of suicidal tendency.

1. The person can fail to develop a sense of a separate identity. His identity may be fused with that of his parents. When intending or wishing to attack the parents, he may then turn his violence onto himself. If he loses a parent through death, he may try to rejoin the loved one by means of suicide.

2. The person's development may be blocked so that he does not learn to control his own behavior, but instead relies on external controls to keep him from getting into trouble. Thus, when an impulse toward suicide is present, the individual has no internal techniques of controlling it (by reminding himself that he is afraid to die, or by concentrating on possible future pleasures, for example). If no one else is present to help him, he may yield to the impulse.

3. The individual may develop only one rigid method of dealing with problems and may lack normal flexibility in handling new situations. When a crisis develops, he is often unable to find a solution, and, in addition, is unwilling to accept compromises. (Further discussion of these three developmental possibilities will be taken up in a later chapter.)

If Leonard's theory were correct, the only developmental period in which there is danger of producing a potential suicide would be the age of one to three years. Once the child passes safely through this period, he would be "immunized" against suicide. We suspect that the development of suicidal tendencies may not be that simple. The remainder of this chapter investigates other ways in which childhood experiences can lead to suicidal behavior.

THE EFFECTS OF PARENTAL DEPRIVATION

An obvious factor to consider when looking at childhood experiences is the loss of a parent through death, divorce, or abandonment. Many research studies have been directed toward finding a relationship between loss of a parent and later suicidal behavior. Unfortunately, the results of these studies are unclear and are in conflict with each other. It appears, after comparing the results of this research, that there is a weak relationship between loss of a parent and suicidal tendencies. People who have lost a parent during childhood are slightly more likely to be suicidal. However, losing a parent is not a simple event, and we cannot expect a simple cause-and-effect relationship here. The effects of the loss may differ greatly depending on such factors as the previous relationship with the lost parent and with the remaining one, the size of the remaining family, and the family's economic situation.

A factor that seems to encourage suicide in persons who lost a parent in childhood is the loss of some social relationship as adults. One theory states that early loss may sensitize a person to later losses, causing his reaction to be unusually dramatic. Other suicidologists prefer the idea that early loss prevents a person from learning how to establish and maintain healthy relationships. He may later become involved in unhealthy relationships that are likely to lead to loss.

THE PARENTAL FAMILIES OF SUICIDAL INDIVIDUALS

What sorts of families do suicides come from? This question covers many factors which are potentially important in the development of suicide—relations between parents, whether a child was wanted, and so on. Because there are so many topics to investigate, little research has yet been done on any single aspect. We will discuss only a few of the studies that have been made.

One investigation (Margolin and Teicher, 1968) looked at adolescent boys who had attempted suicide, and noted some general features of their cases. The boys' mothers had often been angry, depressed, or withdrawn, both before and after their pregnancy, which was usually unwanted. The children frequently experienced some maternal deprivation during the first year of life. The father was often lost by the fourth or fifth year of life, leaving the son with no strong relationships with males. (This period is, of course, considered by psychoanalysts to be the crucial time when the Oedipal conflict is worked out, resulting in the boy's identification with his father's social role.) There was often a reversal of roles between mother and son, with the child acting as the "man of the family" and as its head. The sons functioned socially and emotionally as husbands of the mothers, who they felt did not love them. The suicide attempt often came at a time when the mother was depressed and withdrawn, and when the son felt rejected or threatened by loss of the mother.

Another approach to the study of the suicide's parental family involved the mother's social participation (Teele, 1965). Surprisingly, mothers of suicides seem to be more socially active, more intelligent, more "clear-minded," and more understanding than those of non-suicides. This researcher argued that the more a person's mother participates in social activity, the more the child is exposed to society's ethics and norms, and the more likely he becomes to turn aggression inward rather than outward.

Why is there the apparent contradiction between these two studies? In the first investigation, the mothers of suicides were depressed and unsociable and they forced their sons into an inappropriate role. In the second study, mothers of suicides were sociable, intelligent, and understanding. Superficially, it appears that a mother can't win. It is probable, though, that the seeming contradiction is due to class differences. Margolin's subjects were primarily lower class. The intelligence and sociability measured by Teele would clearly differ with social class.

SIBLING STATUS

The experience of a child in his family may depend greatly on whether he is firstborn, lastborn, or inbetween. The firstborn child may get extra attention from his parents, although the parents may be inexpert at child-rearing. For later children, the parents may be more practiced in child care, but may also be less interested or too occupied by other children to give much attention. The "baby of the family" may retain a dependent role much longer than older siblings may. These differences in childhood experience might lead to differences in suicidal behavior.

Although there is some disagreement on the topic, the majority of research work in this area indicates that firstborn children are more likely to be suicidal than their later-born siblings.

There are several possible explanations for the preponderance of firstborns among suicides. Some researchers (for example, Stanley Schachter) have felt that firstborn children are unusually dependent and have a strong need to be with other people when under stress. Suicidal behavior can be seen as a "cry for help," a way of moving toward or communicating with others. If this concept about suicide is correct, we would expect firstborns to be more frequently involved in suicidal behavior. In addition, if a firstborn had learned inappropriate ways of communicating, he might also be very isolated and desperately crave companionship. His special need for the society of others might interact with his inability to reach other people, with the combination ending in suicide.

Firstborns actually differ from laterborns in many ways, any of which could be responsible for the difference in suicidal behavior. For example, laterborns seem to be physically more vigorous and less hampered by social restraint. Thus, laterborns can more easily direct aggression outward, while firstborns may have to turn it inward onto themselves.

OTHER SUICIDES IN THE FAMILY

Do suicides come from non-suicidal families, or do some families seem to have far more than their share of suicidal members? Clearly, having many suicides in a family could be an experience with a profound effect on a child. He could learn suicidal ways of coping from parents or siblings, or could simply feel that, as a member of a suicidal family, he had an unusually high probability of suicide. (Of course, a high rate of suicide in a family could suggest that the experience itself was irrelevant and that genetic factors were at work. This possibility was discussed in the previous chapter.)

Research seems to indicate some tendency for suicides to have experienced suicidal behavior within their families (although there are some contradictions, as seems unavoidable in this area). It is still not exactly clear how the association works, however. The suicide of a particular family member may be most important for an individual; for example, an eldest daughter might be more affected by the suicide of her mother than by that of her younger brother.

CONCLUSION

Research has yielded contradictory answers to questions about the contribution of childhood experiences to suicide. It appears that family difficulties during childhood make suicide more likely, but the exact character of the difficulties is unclear. Particular punishment experiences and problems in the development of autonomy have been singled out as important factors, as has the experience of loss of a parent. Being the firstborn child and coming from a family where suicide is frequent also seems to predispose a person toward suicidal behavior.

BIBLIOGRAPHY

BELL, R. Q. 1968. A reinterpretation of the direction of effects in studies of socialization. *Psychol. Rev.* 75: 81–95.

GOLD, M. 1958. Suicide, homicide, and the socialization of aggression. *Amer. J. Sociol.* 63: 651–61.

HENRY, A. F., and SHORT, J. F. 1954. *Suicide and homicide.* Glencoe, Ill.: The Free Press.

LEONARD, C. V. 1967. *Understanding and preventing suicide.* Springfield, Ill.: Charles C. Thomas, Publisher.

LESTER, D. 1966. Sibling position and suicidal behavior. *J. Individ. Psychol.* 22: 204–207.

———. 1967. Suicide, homicide, and the effects of socialization. *J. Pers. Soc. Psychol.* 5: 466–68.

———. 1968. Punishment experiences and suicidal preoccupation. *J. Genet. Psychol.* 113: 89–94.

MARGOLIN, N. L., and TEICHER, J. D. 1968. Thirteen adolescent male suicide attemptors. *J. Amer. Acad. Child Psychiat.* 7: 296–315.

McCONAGHY, N., LINANE, J., and BUCKLE, R. C. 1966. Parental deprivation and attempted suicide. *Med. J. Austral.* 1: 886–92.

ROSENBERG, P. H., and LATIMER, R. 1966. Suicide attempts by children. *Ment. Hyg.* 50: 354–59.

SCHACHTER, S. 1959. *The psychology of affiliation.* Stanford: Stanford University Press.

TEELE, J. E. 1965. Suicidal behavior, assaultiveness, and socialization principles. *Social Forces,* 43: 510–18.

TUCKER, G. J., and REINHARDT, R. F. 1966. Suicide attempts. U.S. Naval Aerospace Medical Institute NAM: 1–975.

CHAPTER 6

PERSONALITY DIFFERENCES AND SUICIDE

The term "personality" is used to describe many different characteristics of an individual. It applies to all of the ways he acts that make him different from other human beings. Thus, not all behaviors are counted as part of personality. The fact that a person eats is something he has in common with all living humans and so is not a personality factor. But personality does include how much he eats, what he eats, and when he eats—all factors on which he may differ from many other people.

The foregoing paragraph was written by way of warning, so that the reader will not expect this chapter to concentrate on the psychoanalytic personality components or on the results of psychological testing. Instead, a number of areas of behavior whose relation to suicide has been tested will be examined. These will range from intelligence level to sleeping habits.

SUICIDAL TYPES

First, general attempts to classify types of suicidal people in terms of their needs or motivations will be investigated. Suicide is a very complex behavior, of course, and every suicidal person is different. However, suicidologists have had some faith in the idea that suicide does not occur at random. Thus, they have spent some time trying to define general categories into which most suicidal people can be placed.

Karl Menninger formulated one of the earliest and best known of these classifications. He felt that there were three basic motivations toward suicide: 1. the wish to die, 2. the wish to kill, and 3. the wish to be killed. The person who wishes to die essentially wants to escape from something unpleasant in his life; he may be in a state of chronic physiological or psychological suffering. The person who wishes to kill may see suicide as an act of revenge and as a way of inflicting guilt and suffering on other people. Finally, the suicidal person who wishes to be killed may be seeking punishment for an act or even for thoughts that he considers wrong.

Menninger felt that all three motives played some part in every suicide, although there would presumably be a preponderant motive for every person. It is possible, though, to find suicides who seem to show one primary motive. The following are suicide notes which illustrate the wish to die, the wish to kill, and the wish to be killed.

> Dear Mary, You have been the best wife a man could want and I still love you after fifteen years. Don't think too badly of me for taking this way out but I can't take much more pain and sickness also I may get too much pain or so weak that I can't go this easy way. With all my love forever—Bill. (Shneidman and Farberow, 1957, p. 203)

> Bill, I do hope you'll suffer more than I have done. I wish you'll die in a beer joint. (Wagner, 1960, p. 63)

> Mary Darling, It's all my fault. I've thought this over a million times and this seems to be the only way I can settle all the trouble I have caused you and others. This is only a sample of how sorry I am. This should cancel all. (Shneidman and Farberow, 1957, p. 206).

Shneidman has suggested a very different classification system, based on the source of the suicidal person's problems. He listed three kinds of suicide. *Egotic* suicides are those in which the primary problem comes from conflicts within the person. The person with an egotic suicide pattern may have a strong need for some sort of satisfaction, but an equally strong inhibition against seeking it. *Dyadic* suicides are those stemming from conflicts with other people. *Ageneratic* suicides are those resulting from a sense of alienation, when the individual loses his sense of continuity and participation in the succession of human generations.

Another approach to the classification of suicides involves the description of syndromes rather than single motives toward suicide. Here are a few of the suicidal syndromes which have been described:

1. *The Discarded Woman* (Peck, 1968)
   In this syndrome, the individual feels abandoned, rejected, and finally suicidal after the loss of a loved one.

2. *The Adolescent Crisis* (Peck, 1968)

A young person becomes suicidal in response to family issues, such as those centered around his own dependency needs or attempts to establish a sense of identity.

3. *The Malignant Masochist* (Pretzel, 1968)

The suicidal person in this case has a history of suicide attempts and dedicates much of his life to self-punishment.

4. *The Harlequin* (Pretzel, 1968)

This syndrome is named after the character in medieval drama who is at the same time Death and a seducer. (The concept can be traced back to the story of Pluto's abduction of Proserpine.) The Harlequin is much like the malignant masochist, but in addition he or she personifies and gives an erotic component to the idea of death.

IMPULSIVENESS

In a discussion of personality correlates of suicidal behavior, the consideration of impulsiveness is important. The inability to resist sudden whims could lead to suicidal behavior, just as it could lead to many other rash acts. Students who have attempted or threatened suicide seem to be more irritable and more impulsive than non-suicidal students (Lester, 1967). In a study of people who poisoned themselves but did not die from their act (Kessel, 1966), about two-thirds of the acts were impulsive. That is, although the people had probably thought about suicide at some time in the past, they had not been thinking about suicide immediately before their act. The impulse "just came over them," and they yielded to it at once. Such impulsive suicide attempts are less likely to be fatal than carefully planned ones, which may be partially due to the fact that the impulsive attempter does not really want to die.

ATTITUDES TOWARD DEATH

The many metaphors used to represent death show what differing attitudes toward it are possible for human beings. Death may be seen as an event of total abhorrence, which anyone would avoid as long as possible. It may be seen as a means of escape from an unpleasant life, the way to avoid "the slings and arrows of outrageous fortune." It may be considered as a quiet and dignified exit for those who have lived good lives, but a terror for the profligate. Clearly these attitudes and the multitude of other possibilities will be affected by an individual's beliefs in the existence and nature of an afterlife.

A person's attitudes about death might be expected to influence his readiness to kill himself. Considerable research has been done on the effect of this personality variable on suicidal behavior. A number of research methods have been used: asking subjects to rate the concepts of life and death as positive or negative, giving questionnaires in which agreement or disagreement with statements about death must be estimated, testing physiological responses to words relating to death or suicide, and so on. Unfortunately, although most of the studies have found relationships between death attitudes and suicidal behavior, the results of different studies are mutually contradictory. Some real relationships probably exist. However, correlations may be different for men and women, for people of different ages, for attempted and completed suicides, and so on. As long as studies do not carefully handle these groups separately, it may be impossible to find a consistent relationship between suicide and attitudes toward death.

HOPE

A factor that may be more important than the attitude toward death is the attitude toward life—the degree of hope about the life situation. One suicide researcher has suggested that the suicide is more negative about life than positive about death; that he is

> . . . being driven *from* life, into a state of non-being, which they designate as *not being alive*. At least on a semantic level, it is not so much that the suicidal person is pulled toward death as a positive, desired state, so much as he feels the need to remove himself from a painful and meaningless life. (Ganzler, 1967, p. 95)

M. L. Farber has tried to analyze the degree of hope about life in terms of the "sense of competence" postulated by Robert White. White's idea is that the sense of competence is the basis of all human motivation. Simply put, it is the feeling of being able to make some change in the environment, of being able to control the world, and, by implication, of being sure that the world will satisfy one's needs. In Farber's theory, some personalities may tend to suicide because of a chronically reduced sense of competence. Others will become suicidal when some change in the social environment causes their feeling of competence to diminish. When the latter event occurs,

> the situational factor that contributes to hope in interaction with the sense of competence is the degree of threat leveled against the individual's being able to sustain a minimally acceptable existence. The loss of or abandonment by a loved one, the loss of one's fortune or

position, the ravages of a disease—these are the kinds of threats that place in jeopardy the ability to maintain a minimally acceptable existence. (Farber, 1968, p. 15)

To state this theory in formal terms, Farber has said that

$$\text{probability of suicide} = f\frac{(1)}{\text{hope}} = f\frac{(\text{threat to acceptable life conditions})}{(\text{level of sense of competence})}$$

In other words, the greater the feeling of hope, the less the likelihood of suicide. The amount of hope is increased when the feeling of competence increases, but decreases when acceptable life conditions are increasingly threatened. If a person has a strong sense of competence, a serious threat to his life conditions will be needed before the probability of suicide becomes great. If one starts out with a minimal sense of competence, a trivial threat to life conditions might be enough to make suicide a serious possibility.

Empirical research seems to support Farber's ideas. Suicidal people tend to see not only the present but also the future as negative. In particular, they expect to be socially isolated in the future. Clearly, the expectation of social isolation is a "threat to acceptable life conditions." As such, it could be a factor in reducing hope and leading to suicidal behavior.

SELF-CONCEPT

An important variable in suicide may be the way in which the suicidal person thinks of himself—his self-concept. If he considers himself worthless and guilty, there may be an increase in what Menninger called the wish to be killed. There are a number of ways to determine a person's self-concept. He can be given a list of adjectives and asked to check the ones that apply to himself; he can simply be asked to describe himself; he can be asked to check adjectives that describe how he would like to be, and then compare these to the way he thinks he really is; and so on. These methods have yielded some information about the self-concept of the suicidal person.

A doctoral dissertation by D. H. Miller (1968) explored a number of aspects of self-concept which seem relevant to suicidal behavior. Miller felt that seriously suicidal people are overcommitted to some hero-image which they are unable to emulate but can never abandon. The suicidal person is also unable to communicate well with his loved ones, so the latter cannot help him to deal with his overcommitment. The potential suicide is isolated by his inability to communicate and spends his time deprecating himself for failing to achieve the status he wants. A minor event can then trigger a crisis, if it seems relevant to the conflict the individual is feeling about his ideal self. He may see himself as a failure, as worthless, and as better off dead.

Miller's empirical studies supported these ideas. The suicidal people she studied seemed to be more negative about themselves than non-suicidal people. They were also more rigid and authoritarian, more prone to have crises, and more inclined to have problems in communication.

PRE-SUICIDAL MOOD

Most implicit theories of suicide assume that depression is the immediate forerunner of a suicidal act. This common belief is not supported by the empirical evidence, although, of course, many suicidal people are depressed at some time before the actual suicide attempt. There seems to be a tendency for depression, confusion, and anxiety to clear shortly before the suicidal act, so that during the preceding day or so the suicidal person may appear calm and optimistic. This may be due to an improvement of mood once the decision to commit suicide has been made. On the other hand (as Spiegel and Neuringer have pointed out), it may be that the suicidal person must repress his awareness of suicidal desires in order to be able to kill himself. If he were aware of his suicidal wishes, the fear of death attendant upon considering suicide would make him unable to carry out the act. This mechanism may be responsible for the euphoric mood which may immediately precede a suicidal act.

In severely depressed patients, suicide is much more likely when the person is beginning to recover than when he is at the stage of deepest depression. Suicide is also very common among mental patients who have just been released from the hospital.

FEELING AND BEHAVIOR SYMPTOMS

As the late George Kelly used to say, one of the best ways to find out about a person is to ask him about himself. This statement applies to suicidal behavior as well as it does to other personality disturbances. Symptoms reported by individuals themselves seem to be good predictors of suicide. People who are potential suicides seem to be more likely than non-suicides to have the following symptoms: sleeplessness, agitation, tension, nervousness, worries, marked anxiety, and marked depression. Insomnia in particular has been considered a predictive sign of serious suicidal thoughts. (The problem of sleep patterns as they relate to suicide will be discussed in greater detail below.)

REACTION TO CRISES

Serious suicidal preoccupation may constitute a crisis in itself. However, it often occurs that the suicidal thoughts begin while some other sort of crisis is in progress. Because this seems more than coincidental, some suicidologists have looked into the problem of the suicidal person's ability to handle crisis situations.

The kinds of circumstances that can precipitate suicidal acts seem to differ with the seriousness of the person's preoccupation with suicide. The more seriously the individual is thinking of suicide, the more likely it is that his act will be brought about as a result of conflict with others.

When a suicidal person finds himself in a conflict situation, his emotional responses seem to differ from those of non-suicidal individuals. Male suicides tend to feel depressed or like giving up and to get angry with themselves. Suicidal women say that they feel "burned up or boiling inside" and that they tend to swear and throw things. The men's emotional responses clearly involve inhibition of rage or a turning-inward of the anger. The women's aggressiveness seems more externalized, but when we consider how little violence is culturally permitted to women, we can see how suppressed anger might be turned back onto the self. When a suicidal woman becomes seriously angry, violence to herself could fulfill both a need for expression of the rage and a need to punish herself for her "unfeminine" violence.

MACHIAVELLIANISM

Whether or not it is intended to do so, suicidal behavior can serve to manipulate other people's feeling toward and treatment of the suicidal person. Expertise in manipulating other people, in getting them to behave in the desired ways, has been given the name "Machiavellianism," after the Italian writer who produced a treatise on how a person in power can best control everyone he has to deal with. One research worker (Christie, 1967) has devised a scale to measure this kind of manipulativeness. On Christie's scale, psychiatrists make higher scores than general practitioners, and people who win at poker make higher scores than those who lose.

Little testing of suicidal people for Machiavellian tendencies has been done, but the existing work seems to indicate that people with high suicidal potential also tend to be highly manipulative of others. Of course, this does not prove that suicidal acts are simply or even primarily for manipulative purposes. It could be that people who have learned to get along with others only by manipulating them lead such unhappy lives that suicidal behavior is easily precipitated. However, it must be remembered that (from the viewpoint of others if not that of the suicidal person) self-destructive behavior frequently acts to force changes in the behavior of family and friends.

SLEEPING HABITS

Edwin Shneidman (1964) has looked at sleep patterns and attitudes as they relate to suicidal behavior. His assumption was that sleep can be seen as "a little death"; therefore, there may be some relation between sleeping habits and the decision to try suicide. He found that suicidal persons tended to conceptualize sleep in particular ways—for example, as a temporary death or as "a chance to find oneself." Shneidman also reported that people with serious suicidal tendencies often used sleep as an escape from their problems and tended to have difficulty facing the morning when they woke up. Perhaps these behaviors are related to the data discussed above on insomnia as a predictor of suicide. If seriously suicidal people use sleep as a temporary rest from their problems, and if insomnia prevents them from using that escape route, tension might build up to such an extent that suicide is seen as the only possible surcease.

INTELLIGENCE, PERFORMANCE, AND ASPIRATION

In Chapter 4 the relationship of suicidal motivation to success and failure in Sweden was discussed. Although the problem of performance seems especially relevant to Swedish suicides, we might expect that, in all cultures, ability and success could play an important role in the development of suicidal behavior.

The numerous studies on the relation of intelligence level to suicide have revealed no tendency for suicidal persons to have higher or lower intelligence than non-suicides. (Incidentally, we might expect retarded people to have a lower rate of completed suicide than normals, simply because of inability to solve the problem of how to kill oneself. This has not yet been demonstrated, however.)

Tested intelligence in itself does not reflect how well a person performs. A highly intelligent person who is emotionally disturbed or poorly motivated may not perform to capacity, while a less intelligent person may "over-achieve." The tendency for the suicide rate among students at top-ranked colleges to be higher than that for non-students in the same age range suggests that high performance may be related to suicide. Seiden (1966) looked at the academic performance of undergraduates and graduate students who killed themselves. He found that the undergraduate suicides had grade point averages that were significantly higher than those of the average undergraduate. During the semester prior to the suicide, however, their grades were lower than their previous cumulative average. Seiden felt that the undergraduate suicides demanded too much of themselves. He also suggested that their self-esteem was hurt when they found how much greater was the effort needed to do well at college than in high school. (The graduate students Seiden investigated did not differ in grade average from non-suicidal graduate students. Since the range of grades acceptable for graduate school credit is so small [A to B−], it would be very difficult to demonstrate a statistical difference.)

Another study (Yessler, 1968) has looked at suicide as it relates to performance among military personnel. The findings were similar to those in the college student studies. The men who completed suicide tended to be performing at a high level, while the attempters were performing no better than average.

In addition to the variables of intelligence and actual performance, the level of aspiration of suicidal individuals should be investigated. This concept refers to the kinds of goals the person sets for himself, and his reaction when he succeeds or fails in his attempt to reach them. Although the idea of aspiration level is intended to be applicable to everyday life, it is generally tested in the laboratory. In the experimental setting, goal achievements can be regulated by the researcher. A typical task (used by Vinoda, 1966) might be for the subject to tap with a finger as many times as he can in 15 seconds. The subject is then asked to predict how many times he will be able to tap when he tries the task again. This information gives a measure of aspiration (how much he wants to improve) and also of judgment discrepancy (the difference between his prediction and his actual performance). Vinoda tested attempted suicides and found that they did not differ from a control group on aspiration or on judgment discrepancy. However, they seemed to be inflexible; they did not often change their stated goal, in spite of evidence that they had or had not attained it.

PSYCHOLOGICAL TESTS

The frequency with which psychological tests are used as diagnostic instruments reflects a somewhat misplaced faith in them. Newspaper accounts of the arrest of disturbed persons often end with the pious statement that "X was sent to Blank State Hospital for psychological testing." The implication is that the tests will reveal exactly where the individual's id has come unbolted from his ego, whereupon he can be quickly fastened together again. To argue with this general idea about psychological testing is far beyond the scope of this book, but we can say that research indicates very little usefulness for standard psychological tests in the diagnosis of suicidal tendencies. Behavioral symptoms and personal history seem to be much better predictors of suicidal behavior than any existing psychological test.

CONCLUSION

Suicidologists have described a number of general suicidal patterns or types. They have also looked at the relation between specific personality characteristics and suicidal behavior. To sum these up, we can characterize the suicidal person as unusually rigid and inflexible, with a negative view of himself, lacking in hope, manipulative, and high in scholastic or career performance. His suicidal tendencies are not easily discovered by the use of psychological tests, but are best predicted by examination of behavior patterns (such as insomnia) and feelings (such as anger or depression).

BIBLIOGRAPHY

CHRISTIE, R. 1967. Personal communication.

FARBER, M. L. 1968. *Theory of Suicide.* New York: Funk & Wagnalls.

FARBEROW, N. L., and MCEVOY, T. 1966. Suicide among patients with diagnosis of anxiety reaction or depressive reaction in general medial and surgical hospitals. *J. Abnorm. Psychol.* 71: 287–99.

GANZLER, S. 1967. Some interpersonal and social dimensions of suicidal behavior. *Diss. Abstr.* 28B: 1192–93.

KESSEL, N. 1966. The respectability of self-poisoning and the fashion of survival. *J. Psychosom. Res.* 10: 29–36.

LESTER, D. 1967. Fear of death of suicidal persons. *Psychol. Rep.* 20: 1077–78.

MENNINGER, K. 1938. *Man against himself.* New York: Harcourt Brace Jovanovich, Inc.

MILLER, D. H. 1968. Suicidal careers. *Diss. Abstr.* 28A: 4720.

NEURINGER, C. 1964. Reactions to interpersonal crises in suicidal individuals. *J. Gen. Psychol.* 71: 47–55.

PECK, M. L. 1968. Two suicide syndromes. Paper given at meeting of *Amer. Psychol. Ass.,* San Francisco.

PRETZEL, P. W. 1968. Two suicide syndromes. Paper given at meeting of *Amer. Psychol. Ass.,* San Francisco.

SEIDEN, R. H. 1966. Campus tragedy. *J. Abnorm. Psychol.* 71: 389–99.

SHNEIDMAN, E. S. 1964. Suicide, sleep, and death. *J. Consult. Psychol.* 28: 95–106.

————. 1968. Classification of suicidal phenomena. *Bull. Suicidol.* July: 1–9.

SHNEIDMAN, E. S. and FARBEROW, N. L. 1957. *Clues to suicide.* New York: McGraw-Hill Book Company.

SPIEGEL, D. E., and NEURINGER, C. 1963. Role of dread in suicidal behavior. *J. Abnorm. Soc. Psychol.* 66: 507–11.

VINODA, K. S. 1966. Personality characteristics of attempted suicides. *Brit. J. Psychiat.* 112: 1143–50.

WAGNER, F. F. 1960. Suicide notes. *Danish Med. Bull.* 7: 62–64.

WHITE, R. W. 1959. Motivation reconsidered. *Psychol. Rev.* 16: 297–333.

YESSLER, P. G. 1968. Suicide in the military. In H. Resnik, ed., *Suicidal behaviors.* Boston: Little, Brown and Company, pp. 241–54.

CHAPTER 7

SUICIDE AND AGGRESSIVENESS

In trying to understand suicidal behavior, many research workers have considered suicide to be a form of aggression. If killing or hurting another person is aggression, it makes sense that killing or hurting one's self is also a kind of aggressive act. Some students of suicide have gone beyond this simple analogy, however. They have assumed that most people have about the same amount of aggressiveness, but that people differ in the way they direct their aggressive tendencies. Whether a person behaves suicidally or not is partly determined by the way he is directing his aggressive energies at a particular time.

Freud was the first person to suggest this approach to the problem of suicide. He never considered the psychodynamics of suicide in detail, but he made occasional comments on it in his writings. These comments were stimulated by Freud's considerable experience with suicidal patients and possibly by his personal interest in suicide; he himself once threatened to commit suicide if he were ever to lose his fiancée. (Other evidence of Freud's preoccupation with death is shown in his frequent but incorrect predictions of the date of his own death and in his insistence on continuing to smoke cigars through the many years he suffered from the cancer of the jaw which eventually killed him.) Robert Litman (1967) has collected Freud's ideas about suicide and noted that Freud outlined two stages in the development of suicidal behavior. First of all, some loved object is lost. The emotional investment that had been given to the object of love is withdrawn and reinvested within the self. Along with this reinvestment of feeling, the loved one is recreated as a permanent part of the self, a kind of ideal self. This is called identification of the ego with the lost object; Litman called the process ego-splitting, since an ideal and a non-ideal part of the self are created. Secondly, the individual redirects the aggression that he feels toward the outside world toward himself. He has strong feelings of resentment and anger toward the lost object of his love, but there is no way to express them, since the love object is no longer present. Thus, aggression is turned toward the only remaining representation of the love object: the ideal self. In killing or destroying the ideal self, however, the suicidal person also kills himself.

Psychologists and sociologists have stressed the idea of turning aggression inward upon the self, although they have neglected the process of ego-splitting. Suicide has been seen as an act of inward-directed aggression, as opposed to acts of outward-directed aggression, like homicide. Henry and Short (1954) suggested that inwardly- and outwardly-aggressive people develop because of differences in the ways they are punished as children.

Parents who use love-oriented punishment techniques would be expected by Henry and Short to raise children who direct their aggression inward. When the mother or father disapproves of the child's behavior, the child is punished by threatening withdrawal of love or companionship. The child's natural response to punishment is anger, but he feels he must inhibit his resentment, since showing it might actually result in the threatened loss of love. The child thus learns not to express aggression outward. If we assume that the aggression still exists and must be expressed in some way, we have to conclude that the only direction the aggressive tendencies can take is inward.

Henry and Short would expect parents who use physical punishment to raise outward-aggressive children. Anger expressed by the child toward the parents results, at worst, in a spanking, rather than in catastrophic loss of the parent's love. Thus, the child learns that outward expression of aggression is not totally unacceptable, and he grows up to be a person who turns his aggression against the outer world.

These analyses of inward and outward aggression and their sources sound quite logical. Unfortunately, there is little empirical support for them, and "face validity" of a theory is no substitute for solid evidence. Let us look at some recent research that is relevant to the problem of suicide as a form of aggressiveness.

SUICIDE AS INWARD-DIRECTED AGGRESSION

What evidence do we have that suicidal people inhibit aggression? In one study we inquired about the aggressive behavior of students who had differing histories of suicidal preoccupation. Some had attempted and threatened suicide and others had never considered suicide. When frustrated, students did not differ in the extent to which they attacked others, destroyed objects, verbally abused others, or inhibited aggression. Students with differing degrees of suicidal preoccupation reported similar aggressive habits (Lester, 1967).

One psychological test that attempts to measure the aggressive responses of people to frustration is the Rosenzweig Picture-Frustration Test. This test presents people with a series of cartoons depicting two characters, one of whom is frustrating the other. The subject is asked to write a verbal reply for the victim. The responses to the test can be categorized as extrapunitive (aggression is directed toward the frustrator), intropunitive (aggression is directed by the victim toward himself), and impunitive (nonaggressive responses). Psychologists have given this test to people after they have attempted to kill themselves but failed, and have found no evidence that they respond differently from non-suicidal people who have a similar degree of emotional disturbance. For example, Seymour Fisher and Edith Hinds compared a group of hospitalized attempted suicides with a group of non-suicidal paranoid schizophrenics and a group of applicants for jobs at the hospital and found no differences.

There are many clinical data that support the notion that the suicidal person is actually an outwardly aggressive person. Norman Farberow and his colleagues looked at the case records of a group of psychiatric patients who killed themselves and found that they had been very violent when on the wards of the hospital. They had needed physical restraints more often than the non-suicidal patients and had gotten into more fistfights.

CONCLUSION

It is fairly clear from the research point of view that the suicidal person cannot accurately be considered as an unaggressive or inward-aggressive person. Indeed, suicide may even be associated with attacks on other people. Nonetheless, clinicians who work with suicidal people continue to feel that the hypothesis of inward-directed aggression provides them with a good framework. How can we reconcile this conflict between research evidence and clinical intuition? Perhaps the disagreement is due to the fact that research workers are using too simple a concept when they investigate aggressiveness in general. Dorpat (1968), for example, has suggested that the suicidal person might be characterized by a lack of control over impulses—a more complex possibility than simple aggressiveness. If this were the case, students of the relationship between suicide and aggressiveness would need to study impulsivity as well, in order to come to accurate conclusions.

BIBLIOGRAPHY

DORPAT, T. L. 1968. Loss of control over suicidal impulses. *Bull. Suicidol.* December: 26–30.

FARBEROW, N. L., and McEvoy, T. 1966. Suicide among patients with diagnoses of anxiety reaction or depressive reaction in general medical or surgical hospitals. *J. Abnorm. Psychol.* 71: 287–99.

HENRY, A. F., and SHORT, J. F. 1954. *Suicide and homicide.* Glencoe, Ill.: The Free Press.

KELLY, G. A. 1957. Hostility. American Psychological Association, N.Y.

———. 1965. The threat of aggression. *J. Human. Psychol.* 5: 195–201.

LESTER, D. 1967. Suicide as an aggressive act. *J. Psychol.* 66: 47–50.

LITMAN, R. E. 1967. Sigmund Freud on suicide. In E. S. Shneidman, ed. *Essays in self-destruction.* New York: Science House, pp. 324–44.

MENNINGER, K. 1938. *Man against himself.* New York: Harcourt Brace Jovanovich, Inc.

PALMER, S. 1965. Murder and suicide in 40 nonliterate societies. *J. Crim. Law Criminol. Police Sci.* 56: 320–24.

CHAPTER 8

SUICIDE AND HOMICIDE

The acts of killing oneself and killing another person have many aspects in common. They can both be ways of satisfying certain needs. A person who wants revenge can achieve it by physically hurting someone else or by making the other person suffer guilt over his possible responsibility for a suicide. An individual who wants to be punished can destroy himself directly or gain the disapproval and revenge of society by killing someone else. Murder and suicide may also both be considered as ways of draining off mounting hostility.

Because of these shared aspects of suicide and homicide, some relationship between occurrences of the two acts might be predicted. If the two events are alternative ways of achieving the same end, we would expect them to be negatively correlated; that is, groups of people with a high homicide rate would have a low incidence of suicide, and vice versa. If suicide and homicide are brought about by the same cause (severe frustration from the environment, for example), the rates of both should be either high or low, depending on the particular group of people under consideration. In this chapter, the evidence about the relationship between suicide and homicide will be investigated. We will also examine some of the theories that have been formulated about the relationship of suicide to homicide.

CORRELATIONS OF SUICIDE AND HOMICIDE ACROSS SOCIETIES

The relationship between the suicide and homicide rate in a society appears to depend entirely on the group being studied. Every study seems to have come to a different conclusion. Some researchers have reported that the suicide rate was high when the homicide rate was low, and vice versa, while others found that the incidences of suicide and homicide were either both high or both low. One study found evidence for both conclusions. The Catholic provinces of Germany had a high assault rate and a low suicide rate; the Protestant provinces had a high suicide rate and a low assault rate; religiously mixed provinces had equal rates of both. In France, on the other hand, there was a positive correlation between the incidences of suicide and assault (Halbwachs, 1930).

These very mixed results suggest that the problem being studied is too complex to analyze through crude measures that group people of all ages, cultural groupings, and motivations. For some relatively small groups of people (for example, neurotic, highly-educated, fifty-year-old bachelors living in the United States), the relationship between homicidal and suicidal behavior could be very small, while the correlation could be high for some other equally restricted group.

SUICIDAL MURDERERS

In trying to determine the relationship between suicide and homicide, we can look for differences in the kinds of people who commit each act. Generally, murderers and suicides seem to be different kinds of people, when they are compared in terms of age, race, sex, and so on (Pokorny, 1965).

However, there are occasions when both murder and suicide are committed by a person within a relatively short period of time.

Donald West (1966) studied murderers in England and found that about one-third of them killed themselves after killing their victims. A large proportion of murderers also make unsuccessful attempts to kill themselves, though there is little documentation of this. The suicidal murderer differs from the non-suicidal murderer in many ways. For example, the suicidal murderer is more likely to be killing a spouse or a child and is much less likely to use brutal methods. Infanticides, death pacts, and mercy killings are common, leading West to feel that some suicidal murders were motivated more by despair than by aggression.

However, in other cases there appeared long-standing histories of violent behavior, and West saw these suicidal murderers as individuals with a high level of aggression which may be turned against others or themselves depending upon the circumstances. The following case is typical of those reported by West.

> The offender was an excitable, talkative, boastful man of low intelligence. He was constantly unemployed on account of symptoms of backache, which were considered by hospital doctors to be largely hysterical. He was referred to a psychiatrist and put on a tranquilizer. He was in severe conflict with his wife, and various authorities had been approached to intervene on account of his violence toward her and his children. He was described by a family doctor as 'a pale little man, full of resentments against the world and immensely aggressive.' He so resented interference that when his baby had pneumonia he turned out of the house the doctor who called to examine the child. He was reported to have been so irritated by his baby crying during a fatal illness that he picked it up and threw it across the room. His wife had been seen by social workers badly bruised and with a tooth knocked out following arguments with her husband, and on another occasion he had attacked his wife in a very frightening way in the presence of a social worker who had called about the children.
>
> Six weeks before the murder, the offender's wife finally left the home, and two children remained behind. He made numerous threats that unless she returned he would kill the children and himself. Finally, he did so, leaving behind a note blaming his wife. (West, 1966. Pp. 83–84.)

Combined murder-suicide is relatively common in England, where about thirty-three percent of murderers have been found to commit suicide after killing another person (West, 1966). It appears that the suicidal murderer is a very different sort of person from the murderer who does not subsequently kill himself. The former is likely to kill a close relative, a spouse, or a child. He does not generally use brutal methods like strangulation. Instead, he uses methods that allow him to kill at a distance, like shooting or gas. Perhaps the suicidal murderer, who is killing a loved one, cannot bring himself to carry out the act except at a distance.

Women were much more likely to be suicidal rather than non-suicidal murderers. About forty percent of the suicidal murderers in West's study were women, while only about twelve percent of the non-suicidal murders were carried out by women.

The suicidal murderers did not seem to have killed themselves in order to escape punishment for the previous killing. In many cases, the suicide seemed to have been motivated by despair rather than hostility. Many of the murders involved infanticides, mercy killings, and possible death pacts. There appeared in some cases to have been accidental killings, followed by the suicide of the grief-stricken killer.

An investigator of murder-suicides in the United States found that the relationship between the people involved had been one of conflict (Dorpat, 1966). Often, the murder followed a real or a threatened separation. It was suggested that the idea of separation was so frightening to the murderer that his ability to deal with the world (that is, his ego) regressed to a relatively infantile stage. In this infantile state, the individual finds it hard to differentiate between the self and the object of his love. Thus, aggression produced by the conflict with the beloved person can be directed either toward the self or toward the other. Murder-suicide could also represent an acting out of reunion fantasies. That is, once the murder has occurred, the murderer undoubtedly wishes the dead person could be restored to him. The murder occurred in the first place because of a conflict between love and hate, and the feelings of love are not destroyed along with the person's life. The suicide might then wish to rejoin the person he has killed and attempt to do so by means of his own death.

Findings about murder-suicides in the United States have been somewhat different from those in England. Whereas the English acts usually seemed based on despair rather than hostility or guilt, the American suicidal murderers often seemed to kill themselves because of guilt. One researcher (Wolfgang, 1958) compared wives who had killed their husbands and husbands who had killed their wives. He found that ten of the fifty-three husbands subsequently killed themselves, while only one of forty-seven wives did so. This difference was attributed to differences in guilt felt after the murder. Wolfgang hypothesized that the murdered husbands were more likely to have precipitated their deaths by provoking their wives (for example, by beating them). As a result, the wives would feel that the murder had been justified to some extent and would be less likely to feel guilt, and thus be less likely to kill themselves as self-punishment for the murder.

In Wolfgang's discussion of murder-suicide, he pointed out that it is difficult to tell whether a person who has completed suicide was feeling excessively guilty before his act. However, the murderers who killed themselves in his investigation had fewer records of previous arrests than the non-suicidal murderers. Perhaps this indicates that the suicidal people were more concerned with conformity and obedience to the law. A serious crime like murder might make such people feel unbearable guilt.

In considering the role of guilt in the murder-suicide, we should think about two aspects of conscience or superego: the ability to resist temptation, and the tendency to feel guilt when a rule has been broken. It has been suggested (Henry and Short, 1954) that people who complete suicide after a murder have strong superegos, strong internalizations of society's prohibitions. In killing themselves, they carry out society's rule that a transgressor be punished. However, the internalized prohibitions were not strong enough to prevent the murder in the first place. How could they produce strong enough guilt to cause suicide? An experiment in training dogs with different punishment techniques may be relevant to this human problem (Solomon, quoted in Mowrer, 1960). Dogs were supposed to be trained to avoid horsemeat (which they like) and to eat dry dog food instead. One group of dogs received a smack on the nose when they approached the horsemeat, but before they had a chance to begin eating. These dogs developed a strong resistance to temptation, so that they rarely touched the meat if left alone with it. If they did touch it, though, they showed little emotional reaction (guilt in humans). The other group of animals were punished just after they began eating the horsemeat. They developed little resistance to temptation, but appeared emotionally distressed after "breaking the rule." This experiment suggests that perhaps the punishment process should be studied with respect to aggression. Perhaps murderers who do not commit suicide have been punished as they were approaching outward expression of aggression rather than after the act had begun. They may as adults attack others only under extreme provocation, but feel no guilt afterwards. Murderer-suicides, on the other hand, may have been punished only after the act of aggression had begun.

VICTIM-PRECIPITATED HOMICIDE

In the previous section, it was mentioned that a murder may occur because of the provocative behavior of the person who is killed. One way of achieving suicide could be to antagonize another person so seriously that murder results. In a study of homicide in Philadelphia (Wolfgang, 1959), it was estimated that the victim had precipitated his own murder in twenty-six percent of the cases. Wolfgang felt that the murder victims who had provoked their killers were suicide-prone, but that they differed from ordinary suicides in the extent to which they had internalized the standards of society. That is, the murder victims had weakly developed ethical standards for their own behavior. The guilt they felt on transgression of a standard was diffuse and not clearly felt at a conscious level.

Whether a person completes suicide or provokes someone else into killing him may depend on the subculture in which he lives. If his cultural group allows him more experience of suicides than of homicides, he may choose suicide. Greater experience of homicides may lead him to provoke someone else to kill him. For example, in the Philadelphia study, the white/Negro ratio was 9:1 for completed suicides, 2:8 for victim-precipitated homicides, and 3:7 for ordinary homicides.

THE CHOICE BETWEEN COMMITTING SUICIDE AND HOMICIDE

Although murder and suicide are sometimes committed by the same person, the majority of murderers and suicides appear to be quite different kinds of people. How do people develop into potential murderers or, alternatively, potential suicides? The sociologists Henry and Short (1954) have developed a theory that attempts to explain how one or the other of these aggressive orientations evolves. They assumed that the basic, primary target for aggression is a person other than the self. The self may become the target for aggression, or other people may remain so, depending upon the child's experiences in the course of maturation.

Two sources may be considered as important in determining where the child comes to direct his aggression: sociological pressures and psychological characteristics. In sociological terms, a primary factor may be the strength of external restraint that is enforced on the person. If the child must conform rigidly to other people's demands, the other people share much of the responsibility for the consequences of the child's behavior. If frustration and annoyance occur, it is legitimate and reasonable for the recipient to strike out against other people, who are seen as largely responsible for what has happened. If external restraints are weak, little responsibility can be placed on other people. Thus there is little tendency to attack others when frustrated.

Henry and Short found that there are two psychological correlates of a tendency to orient aggression toward others: 1) low guilt and superego strength ("conscience" or resistance to temptation), and 2) a particular type of cardiovascular reaction during stress. Henry and Short's evidence indicated that, for the male child, these two factors are associated with experience of physical rather than love-oriented punishment, and punishment by the father rather than by the mother. Presumably, other-oriented aggression, which is present from birth, continues if punishment is physical. When punishment involves a threatened loss of love, on the other hand, the child cannot react with aggression against the frustrator. If he does, he risks further or permanent loss of love from his primary source of nurturance.

As mentioned in Chapter 7, there is no research evidence for the assumption that suicide can be seen as an act of inward-directed aggression, although the idea makes good clinical sense. This is a serious problem for Henry and Short's theory. A number of researchers have tested some of the predictions of the theory, however, in spite of this basic objection.

One prediction that can be derived from Henry and Short's theory proposes that suicide should be more common in social groups that have a great deal of freedom of action than in groups in which behavior is seriously constrained by the rest of society. The latter would be expected to commit more murders, since environmental pressure would have encouraged them to assign responsibility to other people and thus to continue to express aggression outwardly. In the United States, murder should then be more frequent among the lower classes and racial minorities, while suicide should be more frequent among the white upper classes. In a study of suicide rates in Cook County, Illinois, the following frequencies were found (Maris, 1967):

Table 8.1

SUICIDE RATES (PER 100,000 PER YEAR)

	White	Nonwhite
Upper Class	15.3	15.0
Middle Class	22.4	14.4
Lower Class	35.7	22.3

Clearly, these results partly oppose what Henry and Short would predict. The suicide rate is highest for the lower class, which is under the greatest external constraint. It would make sense for them to attribute responsibility to other people, since other people often do wield power over them (the factory foreman, the welfare worker, the doctor in the public clinic). However, according to Maris' data, lower class people nonetheless direct aggression toward themselves more often than do members of the upper class. Nonwhites show the same class differences as whites.

The differences between whites and nonwhites are those predicted by Henry and Short. The nonwhites, who have much less social freedom than the whites, have a lower suicide rate. As mentioned earlier, the study of suicide and murder in Philadelphia found a higher murder rate among nonwhites; this too supports Henry and Short's theory.

Another approach to testing Henry and Short's theory involved comparing pairs of groups whose childhood punishment experiences had probably differed (Gold, 1958). It was argued that women were more likely to have been psychologically punished than men, Army officers more than enlisted men, whites more than blacks, and urban dwellers more than rural dwellers. Thus, females, officers, whites, and urban dwellers should prefer the inward-directed modes of aggression (including suicide) to the outward-directed modes (including homicide), as compared to males, enlisted men, blacks, and urban dwellers respectively. All these predictions proved to be correct. (The reader should note that Gold was not looking at the rate of completed suicide alone. Certainly, women do not have a higher suicide rate than men. The question was whether, out of all aggressive acts, suicide or homicide predominated.)

In one last study stimulated by Henry and Short's theory, the suicide and homicide rates in Finland and the United States were compared (Littunen and Gaier, 1963). Previous work had suggested that people living in the United States conform mainly to peer group pressure, while those living in Finland conform more to personal beliefs. In Henry and Short's terms, then, the Americans have greater external restraints than the Finns. The prediction that the suicide to homicide ratio would be lower in the U.S. than in Finland was confirmed. In 1957, the ratio was 2:1 in the U.S. and 10:1 in Finland.

Although the basic assumption of Henry and Short's theory, the idea of suicide as inward-directed aggression, has never been supported by empirical evidence, in many cases it appears that the theory can be used to generate correct predictions. However, we cannot conclude that most of the details of the theory are correct. For example, it could be that external restraints act directly on the adult to cause differences in the ratio of suicide to homicide. There may be no need to theorize about child-rearing practices.

CONCLUSION

Studies on the relation between suicide and homicide rates among large groups of people have given inconsistent results, probably because the phenomenon is a complex one. The occurrence of murder-suicides may yield some information on the relation between the two, but, again, the analysis of these acts seems to give different results, depending on the country. In the United States, guilt seems to play an important role when suicide follows murder. A suicidally-inclined person may also become involved in homicide by provoking another individual to murder him.

Homicide and suicide are comparable in a number of ways, so it is important to find out why some people become murderers and others become suicides. An important theory, which is supported by some research, suggests that homicides have had experience of physical punishment and external constraint, while suicides were psychologically punished and have had fewer external constraints.

BIBLIOGRAPHY

DORPAT, T. L. 1966. Suicide in murderers. *Psychiat. Dig.* 27 (June): 51–55.

GOLD, M. 1958. Suicide, homicide, and the socialization of aggression. *Amer. J. Sociol.* 63: 651–61.

HALBWACHS, M. 1930. *Les causes du suicide.* Paris: Felix Alcan.

HENRY, A. F., and SHORT, J. F. 1954. *Suicide and homicide.* Glencoe, Ill.: The Free Press.

LITTUNEN, Y., and GAIER, E. L. 1963. Social control and social integration. *Int. J. Social Psychiat.* 9: 165–73.

MARIS, R. 1967. Suicide, status, and mobility in Chicago. *Social Forces* 46: 246–56.

MOWRER, O. H. 1968. *Learning theory and the symbolic process.* New York: John Wiley & Sons, Inc.

POKORNY, A. D. 1965. Human violence. *J. Crim. Law Criminol. Police Sci.* 56: 488–97.

WEST, D. J. 1966. *Murder followed by suicide.* Cambridge, Mass.: Harvard University Press.

WOLFGANG, M. E. 1957. An analysis of homicide-suicide. *J. Clin. Exp. Psychopathol.* 19: 208–17.

———. 1958. Husband-wife homicides. *J. Social Ther.* 2: 263–71.

———. 1959. Suicide by means of victim-precipitated homicide. *J. Clin. Exp. Psychopathol.* 20: 335–49.

CHAPTER 9

THE SOCIAL CONTEXT
OF SUICIDE

All of the higher primates have elaborately organized social orders. Relationships between two chimpanzees or two rhesus monkeys in the same group are quite consistent, so that one animal can always be seen to groom or to defer to another. Many non-social behaviors are also determined by the social situation; a chimpanzee may eat only when those animals which dominate him have had their fill, and can sit in a comfortable spot only if that seat is not desired by his "superiors." Human beings, of course, share the stress on social organization that is found in their less developed relatives. Within any group of people who know each other, relationships remain rather consistent over long periods of time.

Suicide, as the act of a human being, cannot help occurring within a social context. No person who commits suicide can be an individual alone in a social void, although he may feel that he is. He has known parents or parent-substitutes; he has worked together with others; he has had teachers and classmates; generally he has had some kind of sexual partner, if only in fantasy; he may have children of his own. The presence and nature of these social relationships and the extent to which the society approves of them, may have a great deal to do with the tendency to suicidal behavior.

MARITAL STATUS AND SUICIDAL BEHAVIOR

The incidence of completed suicide seems to be lowest among married people. It is higher in the widowed and highest of all in divorced persons (Dublin, 1963). (These statements hold for both men and women and for all age groups.)

In widowed persons, the death of the spouse seems to act as a precipitating factor in bringing about suicide. For the first four years of widowhood, the number of deaths from suicide exceeds the number due to all other causes (McMahon and Pugh, 1965). In a person who has any tendency to regard suicide as a solution to his problems, the despair, loneliness, and hopelessness of widowhood may encourage his suicidal preoccupation. If he has defined the spouse as the only person who was a source of nurturance and help, the bereaved person may feel that he has no one to turn to. This may be objectively untrue; there may be many relatives and friends anxious to succor the bereaved one, but as long as he is subjectively alone, he may perceive suicide as the only escape from his misery. And there is, of course, always the possibility that a person who had few social contacts may be objectively isolated after the death of a spouse. In either case, fantasies of rejoining the spouse in an afterlife, as well as the need to escape the pain of bereavement, may lead to suicide.

In divorced persons, the high incidence of suicide has a more complicated background. As with the widow or widower, the divorced person has lost an important source of nurturance. However, the divorcé differs from the widower in that the former's loss was at least in part brought about by a deliberate act of his own. The suicide of the divorcé may be a self-inflicted punishment for the self-produced loss of the spouse. Some investigators of this area have suggested that the divorced person, having suffered a loss as a result of turning his aggression toward the spouse (by means of divorce itself) may tend to turn his anger inward and, in extreme cases, to kill himself (Henry and Short, 1954). Another possibility is that both the divorce and the later suicide stem from some profound unhappiness with the world and that both are attempts to ease the person's situation. It may be that during marriage a person may be able to place all blame for his general unhappiness on the spouse. After a divorce has occurred and the person finds that he is still unhappy, suicide may be seen as the only possible escape.

THE MARITAL RELATIONSHIP
AND SUICIDE

Although the suicide rate is relatively low for married people, marriage does not confer any magic immunity from self-destruction. The occurrence of suicide in married persons provides an opportunity to look at ongoing social relationships as they influence the tendency to suicide. An important aspect of the marital relationship seems to be found in the differences between the suicidal spouse and the non-suicidal partner, especially as far as self-images are concerned (Hattem, 1964). The ways in which suicidal and non-suicidal spouses perceive their own personalities seem to be almost diametrically opposed. The suicidal partner tends to see himself as self-effacing and masochistic, while the non-suicidal spouse sees himself as competitive and narcissistic. These opposing self-images fit well together; the suicidal person has an excellent chance to be self-effacing while his partner is being overbearing and competitive, and the tendencies of the non-suicidal spouse to seek only his own satisfaction are encouraged by the need of the suicidal person to have his desires ignored. In spite of the meshing needs that exist between the partners, the suicidal person often blames his suicidal behavior on his spouse's rejection of him.

The married person who makes frequent, low-risk suicidal gestures may have a special problem within the marital relationship (Peck, 1965). His spouse may tend to communciate in a manner known as "double-binding," in which several mutually contradictory messages came across at the same time. For example, a wife may wear provocative clothing and behave seductively, but become angry and criticize her husband when he approaches her sexually. The double-binding person responds poorly to attempts to clarify the contradictory messages and denies that there is any problem. The spouse of such a person may use suicidal behavior to interrupt and to change the kinds of communications that are coming from the double-binder.

Although the presence and nature of the marital relationship appears to be important in the development of suicide, it remains unclear whether there is a correlation between parenthood (or lack thereof) and suicide. There seems to be some tendency for people who have never had children to have a higher suicide rate than do parents.

GENERAL SOCIAL RELATIONS
AND SUICIDE

The problems of social adjustment that are reflected in the marriages and divorces of suicidal persons are characteristic of their relations not only with their marital partners, but also with people in general. The person who is a high suicidal risk tends to have been unable to maintain warm, mutual relationships throughout his entire life. He does not seem able to express his need to be dependent on and to receive help from others, in spite of the fact that his dependency needs are perhaps more urgent than those of non-suicidal people. The result of this inability to express powerful needs, is, of course, that the needs remain unsatisfied. The lack of gratification is intensified by the fact that even when others go out of their way to be supportive, the suicidal person tends to withdraw from the relationship or to deny that any help is being offered.

Perhaps because of their inability to express dependency needs, suicidal people tend to experience their lives as socially isolated to a greater extent than do non-suicidal persons. There is also a tendency for the suicidal individual to be lacking in hope that his future life will improve and that he will no longer be a social isolate. When he thinks about people with whom he has important relationships, the suicidal person tends to feel that those close friends and relatives feel negatively about him. At the same time, he is much more ambivalent in his own feelings about his companions than is characteristic of non-suicidal people.

Perhaps this expectation of negative feelings from other people and the mixture of negative and positive feelings toward them is based on the suicidal individual's lack of confidence in his ability to handle other people. A number of strategies are available to all of us in our attempts to get what we want from other people. Ganzler (1964) has described some of these strategies as "mature-corrective" (for example, discussing the issue), "positive-manipulative and diplomatic" (such as being affectionate), "distance-producing or avoiding-repressive" (such as staying aloof), "managerial-autocratic and belittling" (such as being bossy), "third-party strategies" (such as making the other person jealous), and "emotional responses and negative feeling" (such as getting angry). Suicidal persons have been found to express little confidence in any of these strategies for controlling interpersonal relations. Particularly, they show much less confidence in the first two strategies mentioned above—the very strategies that are most likely to bring about a lasting solution to interpersonal problems.

SOCIAL RELATIONSHIPS AND THE
SUICIDAL ADOLESCENT

The feeling of social helplessness which is characteristic of suicidal persons in general is probably particularly strong in the suicidal adolescent. Adolescence, at least in American and European cultural groups, is a time of special stress. The young person must break away from his intense childhood involvement with his parents, brothers, and sisters and find a place for himself within the larger society. This is a difficult task at best, and it may be rendered still more difficult by the fact that parents may (for many reasons) resent and oppose the "loss" of their child. Even for the non-suicidal person, bewilderment about how to deal with interpersonal relations is common during adolescence.

Adolescence is not the time of life that produces the highest suicide rate (see Chapter 14). However, adolescent suicides tend to cause great concern to everyone who has been associated with the young person involved. Part of the reason for this may be the awareness of the difficulties of adolescence which is retained by most adults. In addition, the fact that the suicide has occurred at a time when the adolescent was still dependent on his parents may lead the latter to feel that they are responsible for the death of their own child, a feeling that can be the source of tremendous guilt and anxiety. There is also a general attitude that it is very unfortunate for a person to die before he has really had a chance to live. The older suicide, though his act causes grief and consternation among those close to him, may be thought of as having tasted life and decided in favor of death; the adolescent is considered as too inexperienced to have made such a decision. Whatever the reasons may be, we have attitudes of special concern about the suicidal adolescent, and these attitudes have led to special research into suicidal behavior in young people.

One approach to the study of the adolescent suicide has been to look at the kinds of experiences that these teen-agers have had since early childhood (Jacobs and Teicher, 1967). In general, they have a long history of difficulties from early childhood up to adolescence: changes of residence, hospitalization, and other disruptive events are unusually common. Broken homes are no more common among suicidal adolescents than among their non-suicidal peers, but the divorced parents of suicidal adolescents are much more likely to remarry, to remarry unusually soon, and to have an unstable second marriage. After adolescence begins these problems increase even beyond the increase in difficulties that is common for adolescents. Immediately before the suicide attempt, these individuals often experience further disruptions, particularly disruptions of a kind which dissolve whatever few meaningful relationships they might have (for example, the break-up of a romance). The suicide attempt does not occur without warning to others; in fact it is foreshadowed by an escalation of problems between the parents and the child, resulting in still more loss of human contact for the child. Often the child responds to the original difficulties in some relatively adaptive and healthy way (for example, running away from home). The parents respond in negative ways to this attempt to handle problems and tend to be rather punitive, using nagging, yelling, and whipping to an unusually great extent. The culmination of this increased alienation within the family is that the adolescent feels that he has exhausted all possible solutions to his problems and attempts suicide.

A second approach to the problem of adolescent suicides has been to look at how suicidal college students feel about their own social relationships. Some considerable differences exist between the feelings of suicidal and non-suicidal students toward their friends and relatives. Non-suicidal people generally feel that there are some people in their lives whom they can turn to for help. There are also some people whom they dislike and resent. For the non-suicidal person, these two categories of people rarely overlap; if a person is resented, he is not thought of as a source of help, and if he is a source of help, he is not resented. For suicidal students, these two kinds of feelings about other people are much confused. There may be great resentment against a person who is thought of as a source of help. Concomitantly with this, suicidal students tend to have a greater dislike for their parents than do their non-suicidal peers (Lester, 1969).

These findings about the feelings of suicidal students toward important people in their lives lead to an interesting idea about the basic motivation for suicide. Traditionally, people have felt that a suicide attempt was a means for extorting love and attention from other people. According to this view, the suicidal individual has a great need for affection and can get it only by arousing the pity of others by a desperate action. A more recent idea about the motivation for suicide suggests that the suicidal person is actually trying to prove to himself that the world is as cold and unloving as he has always thought it is (Lester, 1968). The suicidal students who were discussed above resent the world and feel that they have been treated unjustly. One of their motivations, which they share with non-suicidal people as well, is to attempt to confirm their view of the world, to consolidate and re-affirm their beliefs about what other people are like. If they believe that the world treats them badly and deserves their resentment, they may seek to demonstrate this by behaving in such a way that other people actually will reject them. Repeated attempts at and threats of suicide tend, in the long run, to have exactly that effect. Although the friends and relatives of the suicidal person usually feel pity and compassion for him at some level, they also have strong feelings of anger, resentment, guilt, and shame. The negative feelings may be particularly strong because it is rarely possible to express them to the suicidal person. Such communication is inhibited by the parent's or friend's fear of precipitating more suicidal behavior. If the suicidal person repeats his threats or attempts over a period of time, the affectionate feelings of those close to him become less and less easy to arouse, and negative feelings become even stronger. Thus, suicidal behavior makes other people feel and act in a rejecting way and proves to the suicidal person that he is right to resent the world. The same process may also serve to validate for the suicidal individual his feelings that he is not worth caring about.

SUICIDE AND THE EXPERIENCE OF LOSS

So far in this chapter we have looked primarily at the kinds of social relationships that are present in a person's life at the time when he displays suicidal tendencies. Another important question involves the kinds of relationships he has had in the past, and the extent to which he has suffered disruption or loss of important relationships. Other losses, as of a job or of some physical ability, may also be important in the development of suicidal behavior. In one investigation of suicide among men, it was found that about seventy-five percent had lost jobs or suffered a loss of income within the few years prior to the suicide (Breed, 1963). Among women, loss of some personal relationship plays a role similar to that of job loss among men. Of course, for any particular man, loss of a person may precipitate suicide, while loss of a job or of income may have the same effect on a woman. But, in general, suicidal reactions to loss among women tend to center around loss of a personal nature, while men appear to be more sensitive to loss of a job or income. This pattern makes sense when we consider that most of a man's social status is dependent on his employment and achievement, while a woman's standing, even today, tends to be derived from her parents, spouse, or children.

It is clear, of course, that many people experience severe loss without becoming suicidal. What is the process that leads a person from loss to suicide? It may be based on changes in the person's attitudes toward himself. To a considerable extent, people's attitudes toward themselves are based on their estimates of how other people feel about them. One's own judgment of himself has much to do with the way one is reflected in the mirror of other people's opinions. Many losses, whether of people or jobs, may realistically imply a rather ugly image in that mirror. Loss of a job or a boyfriend may mean that life will be more difficult and lonely for a while, but it also means that other people have made some highly negative judgments. A person can respond to those negative judgments in several ways: he can change his behavior, he can decide that the disapproving person is wrong, or he can change his opinion of himself in a negative direction. If he takes the last option, the person may lose confidence in himself, communicate the lack of confidence to others, and receive further rejection. The spiral may end with the feeling that there is no alternative except suicide.

CONCLUSIONS

As the reader can see from the examples given in this chapter, good social integration is insurance against suicide. Suicide is far less likely for a person who has lasting, satisfactory, unambivalent relationships with other people than it is for the social isolate or for the person whose closest relationships are permeated with resentment. Loss of close relationships, whether by accident or by deliberate withdrawal, may serve as a signal to a person's friends that the danger of suicide is increasing. Suicidal behavior does not occur without warning, and one of the most accurate warnings is found in the social relations of the potential suicide.

BIBLIOGRAPHY

BREED, W. 1963. Occupational mobility and suicide among white males. *Amer. Sociol. Rev.* 28: 179–88.

DUBLIN, L. 1963. *Suicide.* New York: The Ronald Press Company.

GANZLER, S. 1964. Some interpersonal and social dimensions of suicidal behavior. *Diss. Abstr.* 28B: 1192–93.

HATTEM, J. V. 1964. Precipitating role of discordant interpersonal relationships in suicidal behavior. *Diss. Abstr.* 25: 1335–36.

HENRY, A. F., and SHORT, J. F. 1954. *Suicide and Homicide.* Glencoe, Illinois: The Free Press.

JACOBS, J. 1967. Adolescent suicide attempts. *Diss. Abstr.* 28A: 801.

JACOBS, J., and TEICHER, J. D. 1967. Broken homes and social isolation in attempted suicide of adolescents. *Int. J. Social Psychiat.* 13: 139–49.

LESTER, D. 1968. Attempted suicide as a hostile act. *J. Psychol.* 68: 243–48.

LESTER, D. 1969. Resentment and dependency in the suicidal individual, *J. Gen. Psychol.* 81: 137–45.

MACMAHON, B., and PUGH, T. 1965. Suicide in the widowed. *Amer. J. Epidemiol.* 81: 23–31.

PECK, M. L. 1965. The relation of suicidal behavior to characteristics of the significant other. Ph.D. Thesis, University of Portland.

CHAPTER 10

SUICIDAL COMMUNICATIONS AND THE SUICIDE NOTE

A suicide attempt is the penultimate in communicating to other people that one is unhappy. It is an act whose significance is very difficult to ignore, even though other communications may have been discounted. Many suicidologists have stressed the communicative aspects of suicide attempts much more than the death-seeking aspects. Farberow and Shneidman, for example, called their book on attempted suicide *The Cry for Help.* Even a completed suicide may have its communicative goals. Although the individual will not in reality be around to see the effects of his communication, his motivation toward completing suicide may include an unrealistic feeling that he will get the benefit of the results of his death.

Clearly, there are many ways other than suicidal behavior available for people to use in communication. The suicidal person's other communication channels must be very poor if he is forced to communicate through suicide. The reason for the fouling of other channels presumably lies in the complications of his social relationships, which are discussed in Chapter 9.

In this chapter, we will look at the attempts that are made to use less desperate forms of communication prior to a suicidal act. As stressed previously, suicide is prefigured by many behavioral changes. Attempts to communicate his distress are among the changes shown in the suicidal person's behavior.

HOW FREQUENT ARE PRE-SUICIDAL COMMUNICATIONS?

One group of researchers (Robins et al., 1959) interviewed the relatives of a sample of completed suicides in order to find how and to what extent the suicidal intent had been communicated. They found only one kind of nonverbal communication (a suicide attempt), but twenty-six kinds of verbal communication, ranging from bold statements of suicidal intent, to talk about other people's suicides, to calling up old friends. Some sixty-nine percent of the suicides in the sample had communicated their intent, with the average number of communications per person estimated at about 3.2. Most of the communications had taken place within a year before the death. Of those who had longstanding suicidal communications, a number had intensified their communications within the year. The communications had been made to a wide range of friends and relatives.[1]

REACTIONS OF OTHERS TO COMMUNICATIONS

When friends and relatives receive a suicidal communication, their reactions are varied. In some cases (for example, if the suicidal person is a chronic alcoholic), the reaction may often be skeptical. If the person tends to make unrealistic statements on other topics, his friends and family may take a serious suicidal statement with several grains of salt.

In Robins' study, most people who found themselves the audience of a suicidal communication experienced a rise in tension and anxiety, however. They felt distressed, but did not feel capable either of preventing the suicide or of turning over responsibility to someone else. They often discounted the communications, using the rationale we have mentioned previously, the idea that "those who talk about it don't do it." The hearers convinced themselves that the suicide's mood was temporary. They also began to feel helpless and incapable of dealing effectively with the problem.

[1] Women tended to communicate to their physicians more than men did.

WHY COMMUNICATE?

What motivations lead a person to communicate his feelings to friends prior to a suicidal act? The reason must depend partly on the suicidal individual. Robins' group came up with four possibilities after their interviews with relatives and friends of suicides:

1) The suicidal person was ambivalent about dying and was "crying for help" to others. If we consider the suicidal act itself as a form of communication, we might say that the person tried more and more desperate communications channels until he died in the attempt to communicate. In any case, we must assume that the person who makes suicidal statements is not wholly bent on dying, for he is giving other people a chance to prevent his suicide.

2) The potential suicide wanted to prepare people in his life in order to reduce the shock they would feel when they heard about his death. One might expect that this motive would exist primarily in those who want to die in order to escape some kind of suffering. The motive does not seem congruent with the resentment and manipulativeness which are often characteristic of the suicidal person.

3) The suicidal individual had no desire to die but simply wished to threaten and taunt other people. As was noted above when we described how people react to suicidal communications, the suicidal person may be very successful in this aim. Most people are severely threatened by statements of suicidal intent, and their feelings of helplessness are very unpleasant. Why go on to commit suicide, then, if threats are so effective? There could be many reasons. Family and friends, though originally agitated by suicide threats, may learn to ignore them after a time. Even if their distress continues, the suicidal person may no longer be satisfied by the effect he is achieving. Finally, suicide must be determined by a complex of motives. For example, the suicidal person may begin to feel guilt over his behavior; this, combined with his previous motivations, may be enough to produce suicide.

4) The suicidal person may not really intend his statements as communication. He may be preoccupied with thoughts about death, and his remarks may be a reflection of his concern rather than an attempt to communicate. Clearly, some kinds of remarks ("You'll be sorry when you find me hanging from the shower stall!") can not be attributed to this motivation.

THE SUICIDE NOTE

The one kind of pre-suicidal communication that has become famed through novels and films is the suicide note. This communication, gen-

erally made shortly before the suicidal act occurs, is valuable to suicidologists as well as to novelists. The suicide note is one of the few pieces
of objective evidence available for study after a suicide has been completed. When a researcher must interview family and friends, the information he gets is distorted by memory, if not deliberately censored by
the informant. Sometimes hospital files are available, but even they may
misrepresent the suicidal person. The suicide note alone gives a concrete
sample of the person's behavior soon before his death.

How many people leave suicide notes? The practice is not as universal
as is commonly thought. Shneidman and Farberow (1961), in a thorough
study of suicide in Los Angeles County, found that thirty-five percent of
male and thirty-nine percent of female completed suicides left notes
which were found by the authorities. About thirty percent of these left
more than one note. In cases of attempted suicide, only two percent of
the males and one percent of the females left notes that were found. These
figures are undoubtedly underestimates of the number writing notes. The
attempters could destroy the note before it was found, and the friends or
family of the completed suicide might be reluctant to report a note found
when the body was discovered.

IDENTIFYING A GENUINE
SUICIDE NOTE

Can people tell genuine suicide notes from fakes? This question is important for several reasons. First, if real suicide notes differ from other
written productions, they could cast some useful light on the thought
processes that precede suicidal acts. Second, there are practical implications for being able to identify a genuine note. A murder may be ar-
ranged to look like a suicide, even to the writing of a note—but, if the
note can be picked out as a phony, the real state of affairs will be revealed. Finally, a note left by an attempted suicide could be analyzed in
order to estimate the probability that the person would complete suicide
in the future.

A person's ability to judge whether or not a suicide note is genuine
seems to depend on his experience with such notes. According to Osgood
and Walker (1959), graduate students with no experience of suicide
notes did no better than chance when trying to tell which of a pair was
the genuine note. Out of thirty-three pairs of notes, the graduate students
made an average of 16.5 correct choices. Later, the experimenters themselves read a sample of suicide notes and a sample of ordinary letters for
comparison purposes. After this experience, they chose correctly on an
average of 28.5 of the pairs. Another study (Frederick, 1968) had genuine suicide notes recopied by hand by non-suicidal people. He then

asked graphologists, secretaries, and detectives to judge on the basis of handwriting which notes had been written by suicides. The detectives and secretaries performed at chance level, but the graphologists were able to identify the genuine notes quite accurately.

CONTENT ANALYSIS OF THE SUICIDE NOTE

Rather than having experts judge a note's genuineness in some holistic fashion, it may be possible to develop some means of analyzing the ideas in the note and the way they are expressed. Suicidologists have analyzed suicide notes in terms of the motives implied in them; the emotion that predominates; and the syntactical qualities. There have also been analyses based upon the predictions of particular theories. In this section, we will discuss some of the analyses which have been done, and their results.

J. Jacobs (1967) has taken the point of view that the performance of a suicidal act is not possible until the individual has broken through cultural constraints against suicide. The suicide note may reflect the intellectual and emotional mechanisms used to overcome his culturally-determined bias against suicide. To break the constraints, the person must be in a situation where he:

1. is faced with extremely distressing problems
2. views the situation as part of a long history of similar crises
3. believes that death is the only solution to his problems
4. becomes increasingly socially isolated so that he cannot share his distress with others
5. overcomes his belief that suicide is irrational or immoral
6. succeeds in this because his social isolation makes him feel less constrained by societal rules
7. rationalizes in such a way that he can see the problem as not of his own making or open to no other solution
8. makes some provision that his problems will not recur after death.[2]

Jacobs used four categories of suicide note, based upon the elements from the above group which were contained in the note. The first category contains most of the aspects described above. The suicidal writer begs forgiveness, shows that the problem is not of his own making, notes that the

[2] Precautions that troubles will not recur after death can take several forms. If the suicidal person is religious, he may become an atheist and thus avoid questions of Heaven and Hell. On the other hand, he may seek reassurance that God can forgive anything, even suicide; in his suicide note, he may ask God's forgiveness and request that others pray for his soul. Or, he may develop a belief in reincarnation to the exclusion of more conventional religious ideas.

problems have grown beyond endurance, notes the necessity of death, and finally communicates that he knows what he is doing but is aware that his reader will not understand. Here is an example of this kind of note:

> It is hard to say why you don't want to live. I have only one real reason. The three people I have in the world which I love don't love me.
> Tom, I love you so dearly but you have told me you don't want me and you don't love me. I never thought you would let me go this far, but I am now at the end which is the best thing for you. You have so many problems and I am sorry I added to them.
> Daddy, I hurt you so much and I guess I really hurt myself. You only wanted the very best for me and you must believe this is it.
> Mommy, you tried so hard to make me happy and to make things right for all of us. I love you too so very much. You did not fail. I did. I have no place to go so I am back where I always seem to find peace. I have failed in everything I have done and I hope I do not fail in this. I love you all dearly and am sorry this is the way I have to say goodbye.
> Please forgive me and be happy. Your wife and your daughter. (Jacobs, 1967, pp. 67–68)

In Jacobs' second category of suicide note, the writer has an incurable or painful illness. He is less likely to ask for forgiveness or indulgence, since he feels that the reader will not be indignant at his suicide. The reality of the illness makes it unnecessary for the suicidal person to be as punctilious in his rationalization as he would otherwise be.

In a third category of notes, the writer does not ask for forgiveness or go through the usual giving of reasons for the suicide. Instead, he accuses another person of being entirely to blame for his act. Here is an example of this sort of note, which is usually brief:

> Mary, I hope you're satisfied. Bill. (Jacobs, 1967, p. 69)

A fourth category of note contained notes on instructions or a "last will and testament." These were very impersonal and did not explain the reasons for the suicidal act.

Jacobs reported that of 112 suicide notes he examined, only ten did not fit into one of these four categories.

Another approach to the content analysis of suicide notes has been to look at the variables which differentiate genuine from fake suicide notes. Shneidman and Farberow (1957) noted that the types of discomfort statements were different in the genuine and the simulated suicide notes (the latter being written by non-suicidal people for purposes of comparison). The genuine notes showed more intense feelings of hatred, vengeance, and self-blame. In addition to an excess of discomfort statements of those kinds, the genuine notes had more neutral statements (showing neither positive nor negative feelings). The authors felt that the excess of neutral statements reflected the suicidal person's tendency to give orders. Shneidman and Farberow felt that the suicidal person has unrealistic feelings of omnipotence and in some way expects to be present when the directions in the suicide note are carried out. (It seems equally plausible that the giving of instructions indicates the person's awareness that he is not going to be present.)

Another study has been based on a theory about the events just preceding suicide (Spiegel and Neuringer, 1963). These workers argued that a person does not necessarily commit suicide just because the urge to die becomes stronger than the urge to live. Before suicide can occur, the individual must overcome the fear and dread that arise when death is contemplated. The dread is reduced through a series of defenses, which might include self-deception over the imminent suicidal act, a tendency to avoid mentioning suicide, and a need to concentrate on things other than suicide. In addition, psychotic processes might serve as a defense against fear by disorganizing thinking. When genuine and simulated suicide notes were rated on these characteristics, it appeared that the genuine notes had less explicitness about the suicidal act, fewer mentions of suicide, a greater number of instructions, and greater disorganization. (One might ask, however, why people who are deceiving themselves about their imminent suicide should write suicide notes at all!)

We will describe just one example of syntactical analysis of suicide notes (Osgood and Walker, 1959). The genuine suicide notes were more stereotyped than the simulated ones on several syntactical factors. The genuine notes used fewer different words and also had more repetition of whole phrases. They had fewer adjectives and adverbs (as compared to the number of nouns and verbs), and they had more "allness terms" (like "always" and "never"). In addition to the stereotypy within an individual note, the suicidal writers tended to use words in common. They used more terms of endearment and references to mother than the nonsuicidal writers. The tendency to stereotypy and repetition of words is one that appears in states of intense stress. The use of "allness words" may reflect the tendency of the suicidal person to think in black and white categories. Perhaps it is this habit of thinking in all-or-none terms that makes him feel suicide is his only alternative; he feels that either his life must be perfect or he must die.

CONCLUSION

A suicide attempt or even a completed suicide may be seen as a desperate attempt to communicate. Such acts are almost invariably preceded by more conventional communications of unhappiness and suicidal intent. These communications are often discounted by friends and relatives or serve only to make their hearers feel helpless. When these communications have failed, a completed suicide is fairly often preceded by a last communicative act: the writing of a suicide note. Genuine suicide notes differ in a number of ways from simulated notes written by non-suicidal people, and in the future these differences may help us to a greater understanding of suicide. The genuine suicide note usually has themes of vengeance or of rationalization of the act; it is stereotyped and disorganized, and often avoids explicit mention of suicide.

BIBLIOGRAPHY

FREDERICK, C. J. 1968. An investigation of handwriting of suicidal persons through suicide notes. *J. Abnorm. Psychol.* 73: 263–67.

JACOBS, J. 1967. A phenomenological study of suicide notes. *Social Prob.* 15: 60–72.

OSGOOD, C., and WALKER, E. G. 1959. Motivation and language behavior. *J. Abnorm. Soc. Psychol.* 59: 58–67.

ROBINS, E., GASSNER, S., KAYES, J., WILKINSON, R. H., and MURPHY, G. E. 1959. The communication of suicidal intent. *Amer. J. Psychiat.* 115: 724–33.

SHNEIDMAN, E. S., and FARBEROW, N. L. 1957. Some comparisons between genuine and simulated suicide notes in terms of Mowrer's concepts of discomfort and relief. *J. Gen. Psychol.* 56: 251–56.

———. 1961. Statistical comparisons between committed and attempted suicides. In N. L. Farberow and E. S. Shneidman, eds. *The Cry for Help,* New York: McGraw-Hill Book Company, pp. 129–35.

SPIEGEL, D. E., and NEURINGER, C. 1963. Role of dread in suicidal behavior. *J. Abnorm. Soc. Psychol.* 66: 507–11.

CHAPTER 11

THOUGHT PROCESSES
OF THE
SUICIDAL PERSON

As a person goes through life, his choice of behaviors may depend on the nature of his thought processes. He may make poor choices because he is not good at using logic to solve his problem. This may be because the person is not good at maintaining a logical sequence of ideas, but it is more likely to be due to distortion of the premises (the elements in the thinking process). For example, a person might need to work through the syllogism:

> Some hippies are atheists.
> Some atheists are anarchists.
> Therefore some hippies may be anarchists.

If the thinker made an error in logical deduction, he might conclude that all hippies are definitely anarchists. Such a logical error, if it were applied to a problem in personal behavior, would yield a poor choice of how to behave. A second (and more likely) kind of error is distortion of the premises so that the terms include more or less than was originally intended. The thinker might distort the term "hippies" to mean all students or all men with beards. He might distort the term "anarchists" to mean "people who are primarily interested in raping nuns." With these distortions, even a logically correct conclusion would have a totally incorrect meaning. This sort of distortion can occur readily with material that is highly personal and emotionally loaded.

Suicidologists have made some studies of both these distortions of the thought process: disordered logic and altered conceptualization of material.

PARALOGIC

One type of logical error ("paleologic" or "paralogic") has been thought common in schizophrenic reasoning. This error occurs in the following kind of syllogistic reasoning:

All As are Bs.
All Cs are Bs.
Therefore, all As are Cs.

The person who makes this error assumes that there are no Bs other than As and Cs. Von Domarus, who originally described paralogic, gave this example of the flaw in schizophrenic thinking:

The Virgin Mary was a virgin.
I am a virgin.
Therefore, I am the Virgin Mary.

Shneidman and Farberow (1957) felt that this kind of logical error may play a part in the reasoning of psychotic suicides, but that it is not found in suicides in general.

DISTORTION OF IDEAS AND PREMISES

There are several ways in which a suicidal person's thinking can be distorted, other than the making of paralogical errors. His thinking may be dichotomous; it may be rigid; it may use single terms ambiguously, although all other ideas are correctly used.

Dichotomous thinking involves the use of extreme value systems. It is thinking in terms of black and white, with no shades of grey. This kind of thinking was mentioned in discussing suicide notes in Chapter 10. The suicidal person may feel that there are only two possibilities for him: a perfect life, or death. We assume, of course, that dichotomous thinking would not apply to the question of life or death alone, but that it might be found in all decisions made by the suicidal person.

Dichotomous evaluative thinking has been studied by Neuringer (1961, 1967), using the Semantic Differential test. The Semantic Differential requires the subject to rate abstract ideas (such as democracy, love, and life) on scales which superficially seem quite irrelevant (good–bad, dirty–clean, happy–sad, etc.). The subject can rate the concept as very bad, moderately bad, mildly bad, mildly good, moderately good, or very good, for example. On the surface, this task seems somewhat absurd; but subjects can perform it, and the results are fairly consistent rating patterns for various concepts.

Neuringer had his subjects rate individually a number of concepts that could be paired into opposites (life–death and honor–shame, for example). If the ratings of the opposites were mirror images of each other, the person was considered as thinking dichotomously. (Life and death would have mirror image ratings if life was rated very good, very clean, and very happy, while death was rated as very bad, very dirty, and very sad.) Neuringer found that suicidal people had the most extreme dichotomous thinking, while normals had the least; people who were emotionally disturbed but non-suicidal fell in between.

Neuringer (1964) also looked at rigid thinking in suicidal people. His primary means of testing rigidity was by means of an attitude test, the California F-Scale. This test asks questions about political, religious, and social opinions, and is based on the idea that people who have unusually conservative opinions are rigid thinkers, that is, incapable of changing preconceived ideas in the face of new information. The F-Scale is known to be correlated with other measures of rigidity. For example, people who score high on the F-scale seem rigid on a reversible-figure test. A flexible observer sees the reversal occur frequently, while those who are considered rigid see infrequent reversals.

Neuringer found that suicidal people scored as rigid thinkers, although other emotionally disturbed people did not. It is logical that inflexible habits of thinking could lead to suicide. Once the rigid thinker oriented himself toward suicidal behavior, once he reacted with severe distress to the circumstances of his life, his ideas and feelings might be impossible to change, no matter how his life itself might alter. The rigid character of the suicide's thought is expressed in the suicide note, where (as is mentioned in the previous chapter) the words "all" and "none," "always" and "never" are frequently found. To a suicidal person, a few instances of a relative's behavior may be sufficient to produce a rigid idea of how the person "always" behaves. Once the idea is present, no amount of changed behavior may be enough to change the conception. Indeed, rigidity of thinking may work together with other characteristics of the suicidal person to produce a rigid picture of a loved one which is far from realistic.

"Catalogic" is the name give by Shneidman and Farberow (1957) to an error that they consider frequent in suicidal thinking. Catalogic is the ambiguous use of a specific term, most commonly the concept of "self." In particular, the suicidal person confuses the self as he experiences himself and the self as experienced by other people. The following argument is an example of catalogic:

> If anyone kills himself, he will get attention.
> I will kill myself.
> Therefore, I will get attention.

Shneidman and Farberow felt that catalogic is a common error in considering one's own death.

> Parenthetically, we believe that this kind of confusion or ambiguity might indeed occur whenever an individual thinks about his death, whether by suicide or otherwise. It may arise because an individual cannot imagine his own death, his own cessation of experience, a state where there is no more self as experienced by the self after death. (Shneidman and Farberow, 1957, p. 33.)

There could be several exceptions (Shneidman and Farberow have noted) to the general idea of catalogic as an error that can lead to suicide. Suicide could occur in the absence of catalogic if certain other unusual situations were present.

1. Some suicidal individuals actually want nothingness and nonexistence. Their suicidal intent may be based on the need to escape from pain. Shneidman and Farberow called these "surcease" suicides. Such people would not be making the catalogical error.
2. Some people believe in a life after death, in which they will continue to experience the self. However, not all such beliefs allow that the individual will be cognizant of events on earth after death; if the belief does not allow this, catalogic could still occur.
3. Some persons may place their highest stress on the self as it is experienced by others. The kamikaze pilots of World War II would be a good example of this value system. The snuffing out of their self-experience was considered as nothing compared to the glory given their memories by their families and compatriots. Shneidman and Farberow called such people "cultural" suicides.

Shneidman and Farberow looked for evidence for their reasoning about catalogic in suicide notes. They felt that catalogic would be shown in the notes through

1) concern with minor details, trivia, and neutral statements
2) concern with the indirect and direct reactions of others

3) lack of concern with the person's own suffering and pain
4) lack of indication of belief in an afterlife.

Their interpretation of the excess of neutral statements in suicide notes was this:

> We interpret the large number of neutral statements on the part of the genuine-note writers as indicative of unrealistic feelings of omnipotence and omnipresence on the part of the suicidal individual. He cannot successfully imagine his own death and his own complete cessation. It also epitomizes the illogicality of the entire suicidal deed—thinking simultaneously and contradictorily of being absent and of giving orders as though one were going to be present to enforce them. (Shneidman and Farberow, 1957, p. 39)

As pointed out in another chapter, however, it may not be so illogical to give orders when one will not be present to enforce them. If the person were not aware that he would not be present after death, he would not need to give orders at all; he could assume that he could be there to arrange his own funeral.

CONCLUSION

Suicidologists have wondered whether suicidal individuals think themselves into suicide because distorted thought processes make suicide seem the appropriate choice of behaviors. Some research has been done on disordered deductive reasoning (paralogic), but it seems unlikely that most non-psychotic suicides are due to this kind of error. It seems more probable that disordered thinking in the suicidal person is a matter of distortion of ideas rather than logic. The ideas of the suicidal person seem rigid and are conceptualized in dichotomous fashion; everything is black or white, with no shades of gray. The suicidal person may also have distortions of specific concepts, for example, the concept of the self.

BIBLIOGRAPHY

NEURINGER, C. 1961. Dichotomous evaluations in suicidal individuals. *J. Consult. Psychol.* 25: 445–49.

———. 1964. Rigid thinking in suicidal individuals. *J. Consult. Psychol.* 28: 54–58.

———. 1967. The cognitive organization of meaning in suicidal individuals. *J. Gen. Psychol.* 76: 91–100.

SHNEIDMAN, E. S., and FARBEROW, N. L. 1957. *Clues to suicide.* New York: McGraw-Hill Book Company.

VON DOMARUS, E. 1944. The specific laws of logic in schizophrenia. In J. S. Kasanin, ed. *Language and thought in schizophrenia.* New York: W. W. Norton & Company, Inc.

CHAPTER 12

SEX DIFFERENCES IN SUICIDAL BEHAVIOR

Of all that is known about the phenomenon of suicide, there is little so clear as the fact that men and women differ in their suicidal behavior. Many studies have shown that the rate of completed suicide is higher for men than for women, but that women show a higher incidence of attempted suicide than men do. These generalizations seem to hold for both adults and adolescents, for people of different races, and in other countries as well as in the United States. Edwin Shneidman and Norman Farberow, studying suicidal behavior in Los Angeles for the year 1957, found that of 768 completed suicides, 540 were by males and 228 by females. Of 2,652 attempted suicides, 1,824 were by females and 828 by males.

Men and women also seem to differ in the seriousness of their suicidal behavior. Not all ways of attempting suicide carry the same possibility of death. It is possible to rate attempts according to their potential lethality. For example, a gunshot wound in the head is very likely to cause death. Taking an overdose of aspirin is much less likely to be fatal, because it is difficult to swallow enough aspirin without causing vomiting. Cutting the wrists is also unlikely to be lethal, because pain prevents the individual from making a deep enough cut. (The recent Czech film, "Closely Watched Trains," contains a scene showing the lengths to which a person must go in order to cut his wrists deeply enough to cause severe bleeding.) Men tend to use the more lethal and women the less lethal methods.

Within each of the possible methods of suicide, there can be more and less dangerous attempts. A person can shoot himself through the heart, or just through a couple of ribs; he can take thirty tranquilizer pills or five. When men and women are compared in terms of the severity of their suicide attempts, most evidence suggests that men make the more severe attempts. The actual difference may be even more extreme than research has suggested, since very mild suicide attempts (which are most likely to be made by women) may never come to the attention of the authorities.

The evidence for sex differences in suicide is thus rather clear cut. What are some of the explanations which have been offered for these differences?

DIFFERENCE IN MANIPULATIVE INTENT

E. Stengel has suggested that women attempt suicide more than men because they use suicidal behavior as a means of manipulating relationships. Other means of pressure, like sheer physical power or financial threats, are not available to women to the same extent that they are to men. The suicide attempts, then, are not real flirtations with death, but rather ways of bringing about change in the environment. Suicidal behavior may, among other things, be an effective way of expressing aggression. The latter idea seems reasonable, but there is as yet little empirical evidence to support it.

DIFFERENCES IN CHOICE OF METHOD

One explanation for sex differences in suicide has been that women are less successful because they choose less lethal methods. Indeed, in the Los Angeles study by Shneidman and Farberow, mentioned above, it was rather clear that the suicide methods chosen differed for men and for women. Only fourteen percent of the women who completed suicide shot themselves in the head, while thirty-five percent of the men did so. Women tend to prefer barbiturates and poisons, or to shoot themselves in the body. As was pointed out earlier, these methods are less likely to be fatal than some others.

However, the difference in the choice of method is not the whole answer. Even when the method is held constant, men are more likely to succeed in killing themselves than women. For example, among the suicides investigated by Shneidman and Farberow, sixteen of twenty-four men who jumped from high places succeeded in killing themselves. Of twenty-seven women using the same method, only nine died.

Perhaps the difference in choice of method, or in success in use of a particular method, is due to differences in values held by men and women. Research into sex differences in attitudes toward death (Diggory and Rothman, 1961) has suggested that women are more concerned than men with what happens to their bodies after death. Perhaps the greater concern of women with bodily appearance is extended to appearance after death. Women might then try to choose the method of suicide which would be least disfiguring to them. Clearly, barbiturates would be less disfiguring than a gunshot in the head or the effects of a fall from the tenth story of a building. However, the less disfiguring possibilities are almost always less lethal as well.

PHYSIOLOGICAL DIFFERENCES

One relevant difference between men and women may be their differing physical strength. Women, being smaller and less muscular than men, may find it more difficult to handle the mechanical manipulations required by the more lethal suicide methods. Firing a gun accurately, plunging a knife, or kicking away a chair may all be more difficult for a woman than for a man, and thus less likely to be performed in a manner leading to death. Lack of physical strength may also lead women to choose suicide methods that require little exertion, like barbiturates and poisons.

A more basic difference, of course, lies in the type and level of sex hormones present in the body. Most research on this topic has attended to relations between hormone levels and suicide in women rather than in men. The sex hormone level in men, of course, is fairly constant over a period of several years. Women, on the other hand, provide excellent subjects for this kind of research, because in almost all women of childbearing age there are considerable changes in hormone levels over short periods of time. These changes are fairly accurately reflected by the simple index of the menstrual cycle. Between the beginning of menstruation and the time of ovulation, halfway through the cycle, there is a low progesterone level and a gradually increasing level of estrogen. Following ovulation, estrogen production is decreased, and the progesterone level rises abruptly, to be maintained at a high level until the next menstruation begins.

There is some evidence that the suicide rate in women differs with the stage of the menstrual cycle. It appears that the most common times for suicidal acts by women are the time of ovulation, the bleeding phase, and the days just prior to menstruation. In pregnant women, who have a high progesterone level, the suicide rate is quite low, only about one-sixth the expected rate. (Obviously, however, it can be argued that there are many factors other than hormone level that could be militating against the suicide of a pregnant woman. Becoming pregnant might in some ways serve purposes similar to those of attempting suicide. For example, pregnancy may attract other people's attention and solicitude. It also leads to a new social role which may, in some cases, be more satisfying for the woman than her old role.)

There is no direct evidence for a relationship between hormone level and suicidal behavior. No one has tested for precise hormone level at the time of suicidal acts. However, Bonciu et al. (1964) performed autopsies on a number of suicides and found that almost all of them had endocrine disorders. Ninety-eight percent showed evidence of thyroid disturbance (the thyroid is intimately related to the bodily conditions that determine proper sex hormone functioning). There was also evidence of ovary dysfunction in the women of child-bearing age. F. J. Kane and his colleagues have reported using Enovid, the synthetic hormone contraceptive pill, to ameliorate the symptoms of a woman patient who was suicidal and psychotic.

In subhuman animals, there is known to be a close association between sex hormone levels and aggression toward others. High levels of male hormone are generally associated with a high level of aggressiveness. The same statement cannot be made of the female hormones, though the hormones which bring about lactation may be associated with aggressiveness in guarding the young from intruders. These relationships between hormones and aggressive behavior, as well as the evidence with a more direct bearing on suicide, suggest that the area of endocrine functioning may be a very important one for suicidologists to investigate.

PSYCHOLOGICAL DIFFERENCES

Some bizarre psychological explanations have been offered for the difference in suicidal behavior between men and women. Davis, in 1904, suggested that the difference was due to differing strengths of religious faith in men and women. However, it is difficult to see why the religious faith of women, which presumably should keep them from completing suicide, should also lead them to frequent suicide attempts.

A more pertinent hypothesis about sex differences in suicidal behavior has come from Leonard Berkowitz's work on aggression. Suicide, of course, can be seen as an act of self-directed aggression. As was mentioned above, in most species of animals, males are more aggressive than females. (The level of aggressiveness in subhuman species seems closely related to the level of the male sex hormone.) In humans, too, research seems to indicate that males are the more aggressive sex, whether aggression is measured by psychological tests or by overt behavior.

Cultural norms generally demand that women inhibit their aggressiveness more than men do. A woman may express hostility by covert verbal attack or by gossip, but is generally expected not to fight physically with an opponent. Her opportunities for expressing aggressiveness are much more roundabout than those that men are allowed to use. A woman is shamed and disapproved of if she is too obvious in verbal attack or if she comes to physical blows with another person. Since women form their attitudes partly through modeling themselves upon other women in the same culture, their aggressive behavior may be inhibited even before the motivation enters consciousness. Fear of shame may be a powerful inhibitor, but introjection of cultural norms may be even stronger.

Berkowitz has suggested that only aggression outward is inhibited. Turning aggression toward the self is one way of inhibiting its outward expression. Since women also tend to have stronger affiliative needs than men, they could satisfy two kinds of needs through attempting suicide. First, they could eliminate the aggressiveness which cultural norms force them to inhibit, and second, they could use the act to bring themselves into more intimate contact with other people. Completing suicide would be of use only for the first motivation.

CONCLUSION

It seems clear that men complete suicide much more frequently than women do, while women make the majority of unsuccessful suicide attempts. These differences appear related to differences in choice of method, but the sex differences persist even when the same method is used. Both physiological and psychological factors seem to be involved here. Hormonal differences and cultural prohibitions on aggressiveness may also be especially important.

BIBLIOGRAPHY

BERKOWITZ, L. 1961. *Aggression*. New York: McGraw-Hill Book Company.

BONCIU, C., BELIS, V., and PETROVICI, M. 1967. The role of endocrine glands in influencing suicide. *Acta Med. Leg. Soc.* 17: 99–117.

DALTON, K. 1959. Menstruation and acute psychiatric illness, *Brit. Med. J.* 1: 148–49.

DAVIS, F. B. 1968. Sex differences in suicide and attempted suicide. *Dis. Nerv. Sys.* 29: 193–94.

DIGGORY, J. C., and ROTHMAN, D. Z. 1961. Values destroyed by death. *J. Abnorm. Soc. Psychol.* 63: 205–10.

KANE, F. J., DALY, R. J., WALLACH, M. H., and KEELER, M. H. 1966. Amelioration of premenstrual mood disturbance with a progestational agent (Enovid). *Dis. Nerv. Sys.* 27: 339–42.

LESTER, D. 1969. Suicidal behavior in men and women. *Ment. Hyg.* 53: 340–45.

MCKINNON, L., MCKINNON, P., and THOMPSON, A. D. 1959. Lethal hazards of the luteal stage of the menstrual cycle. *Brit. Med. J.* 1: 1015.

RUBENSTEIN, R., MOSES, R., and LIDZ, T. 1958. On attempted suicide. *Arch. Neurol. Psychiat.* 79: 103–12.

SHNEIDMAN, E. S., and FARBEROW, N. L. 1961. Statistical comparsions between committed and attempted suicides. In N. L. Farberow and E. S. Shneidman, eds. *The Cry for Help.* New York: McGraw-Hill Book Company, pp. 19–47.

STENGEL, E. 1964. *Suicide and Attempted Suicide.* Middlesex, England: Penguin Books Ltd.

TONKS, C. M., RACK, P. H., and ROSE, M. J. 1968. Attempted suicide and the menstrual cycle. *J. Psychosom. Res.* 11: 319–27.

WHITLOCK, F. A., and EDWARDS, J. E. 1968. Pregnancy and attempted suicide. *Comp. Psychiat.* 9: 1–12.

CHAPTER 13

SPECIAL GROUPS OF PARTICULAR CONCERN TO SUICIDOLOGISTS

In most of this book, we have examined the occurrence of suicide in terms of averages derived from many cases. As pointed out in the preface, this is necessary because specific suicidal people differ from each other in many respects. In order to determine the basic characteristics held in common by all suicides, we need to combine information about many people.

Unfortunately, this approach may lead us into trouble. Although we cannot believe that every suicidal person is different from every other one, it may be that suicidal behavior in some groups of people differs from that in other groups. Groups may differ in their motivations, circumstances, incidence, or manner of suicide. (We have noted some evidence that there are such differences in Chapter 14.) If all groups are viewed together, the special factors involved in suicidal behavior will be lost.

Interest has developed in the suicidal behavior of the population's subgroups. There is particular interest in subgroups in which suicide is considered especially tragic (due to inequities of society), or in which it is becoming increasingly common in recent times. In this chapter, three important minority groups will be considered: young people, blacks, and American Indians. In each of these groups, suicidal behavior differs from that found in the total general population.

SUICIDE AMONG THE YOUNG

Among most groups of people, youth provides a relative immunity against suicide. Self-destructive behavior increases with advancing age. When suicides do occur among the young, however, they are considered especially deplorable, perhaps because the young person is seen as "having everything to live for." Another cause for concern with adolescent suicide has to do with the fact that suicide rates among the young are currently higher than they were ten or twenty years ago. Suicide, indeed, is one of the leading causes of death among young people over fourteen years old (see Table 13.1). It has become so only in recent years.

Table 13.1
LEADING CAUSES OF DEATH, AGES 15–24, UNITED STATES, 1964 (AFTER SEIDEN, 1969)

Cause for death	15–19 years of age		20–24 years of age	
	Rate per 100,000	Rank	Rate per 100,000	Rank
Accidents	53.5	1	66.4	1
Malignant neoplasms	7.7	2	9.2	3
Cardiovascular-renal disease	5.7	3	10.0	2
Homicide	4.3	4	8.8	4
Suicide	4.0	5	8.4	5

Four percent of all deaths of those aged fifteen to nineteen are due to suicide, as compared to 0.2 percent of deaths of those over seventy-five years of age. These unnecessary deaths among the young people, on whose talents the future of society depends, are a real source of concern.

Aside from these special reasons for concern, adolescent suicide attracts research interest because of the ways in which it differs from suicide in the general population. One of the important differences becomes apparent when the statistics are categorized along racial lines. In the last fifty years, suicide rates for all young people (regardless of race or sex) have been below those for the general population. In the last ten years, however, the rate for young nonwhite males has been rising rapidly, so that it is now above the overall average rate for the population. This is a special problem for a subgroup of adolescents, and we will examine it in detail later in this chapter.

Over the entire population, suicide rates are lower among married than among single, widowed, or divorced people. This difference is usually attributed to the effects of social isolation as opposed to those of supportive companionship; in addition, it may be said that persons with suicidal tendencies are less likely to marry (or to stay married). Among young people, however, the situation is strikingly different. The suicide rate for married people under the age of twenty is considerably higher than for single people. Tables 13.2 and 13.3 show the differences that exist.

Table 13.2
COMPLETED SUICIDE RATES PER 100,000
FOR PEOPLE OVER FOURTEEN YEARS OF AGE, SEATTLE, 1948–52
(AFTER SCHMID AND VAN ARSDOL, 1955)

Completed suicide rate	
Total	25.1
Single	29.2
Married	19.3
Widowed	25.7
Divorced	64.3

Table 13.3
DEATH RATES FROM SUICIDE PER 100,000 BY MARITAL STATUS
AND SEX, UNDER TWENTY YEARS OF AGE, UNITED STATES, 1949–51
FROM SEIDEN, 1969

Sex	Total	Single	Married	Widowed	Divorced
Males	0.9	0.9	6.2	0	14.5
Females	0.4	0.3	3.1	9.1	13.8

In the cases reported in Tables 13.2 and 13.3, the reversal of suicide rates for single and for married people (compared to those in the population over twenty-four years of age) is quite clear. The reason for the reversal is more obscure. Perhaps, people who marry young do so to escape from the unhappy homes that are frequently part of the background of suicidal individuals. On the other hand, it may be that the intimacy of marriage creates unusual stresses in spouses who are very young.

In the general population, as stressed before, there is a strong tendency for women to attempt suicide more often than men do, and for men to complete suicide more often than women do. This tendency holds for adolescents, too, and is, in fact, exaggerated among young people. The sex ratio for attempted suicides in the total population has been estimated as females 3:1 over males (Mintz, 1964), whereas the ratio is 9:1 in adolescents (Balser and Masterson, 1959).

What are the causes of suicidal behavior among young people? Among the general population, suicide is associated with ill health, marital conflict, job loss, and so on. All of these are less likely to affect the young person than the older one. Some other factors, peculiar to youth, may influence suicidal behavior in the adolescent.

When puberty begins, the young person is rather abruptly faced with a number of problems he has never had to deal with before. He must control his new sexual impulses and either suppress them or direct them to socially-approved outlets. He must also develop behavior patterns that are appropriate for his sexual identity. Earlier in his life, the individual had to perform a part of this latter task; he had to learn to dress and play like a boy or like a girl. When sexual maturity arrives, the American adolescent has the difficult problem of learning to behave sexually like a man or woman, at a time when very little practice at sexual expression is permitted. Adolescent suicide may be based on guilt, confusion, or despair resulting from failure to perform these difficult tasks properly.

Sexual impulses may also lead to suicidal behavior as a kind of erotic activity. McClelland (1963) has suggested that many women's attitudes toward death are colored by a "Harlequin complex"—a feeling of excitement, of the thrills of flirtation, connected with fantasies about death. Death is personified and is seen as a mysterious lover who will steal away the woman and seduce her. Sexual fantasies connected with death may lead to suicide attempts among adolescent girls who are trying to cope with their sexual desires in a socially-acceptable way.

Among young men, too, suicide may be sexualized in one specific way: death by hanging during erotic fantasies. The erotic component may involve masturbation, or it may be connected with transvestite activity, as seen in hangings where a boy is found dressed in female clothing, sometimes with his hands and feet bound (Stearns, 1953). In many such incidents, death may occur "accidentally" in the course of repeated self-hangings for the purpose of erotic stimulation.

Suicide among college students is a special case with its own problems about the motivation for self-destruction. A number of studies have indicated that suicide is more frequent among students at prestige universities than among non-students of the same age. (Suicide rates of all college students resemble those of non-students of the same age, however.) Table 13.4 shows some differences in suicide rate at British universities of different calibers, as compared to the rate of the general population.

One relevant factor in student suicide seems to be the feeling of success or failure in school. Student suicides tend to have relatively high grade averages, as compared to non-suicidal students (Seiden, 1966). Nevertheless, according to their families, the suicidal students never felt that they were competent or secure in their academic success. They felt that their high grades were an accident and an erroneous indication of their real ability. Munter (1966) called this feeling the "Fraud Complex."

Perhaps the "Fraud Complex" explains the differences in suicide rates at British universities. The highly competitive, highly selective universities have a much higher rate than those with lower standards. Bright students may be more likely to feel that they are failures when they come into competition with others who give them a real challenge. When the bright student is a "big frog in a little pond," objective comparison of himself with his less competent fellow students may be enough to make him feel capable.

Table 13.4
SUICIDE RATES AT BRITISH UNIVERSITIES (AFTER LYMAN, 1961, P. 219)

Populations	Annual suicide rate per 100,000 population, ages twenty to twenty-four
England and Wales	4.1
Oxford University	26.4
Cambridge University	21.3
University of London	16.3
Seven unnamed British universities	5.9

In recent years, the use of drugs has been suspected as a factor in student suicides. As explained in Chapter 16, however, there is no real evidence of a causal relationship between drug use and suicide. If the two are found together, it may be that both are attempts to reach the same goal. Both suicide and the use of drugs can be means of escaping from intolerable situations.

Some of the indicators that suicide is about to occur are the same for younger and older people. Some, however, are most likely to occur in adolescents. Seiden (1969) has compiled a list of symptoms of impending adolescent suicide:

eating disturbances or loss of appetite (anorexia)

psychosomatic complaints

insomnia

withdrawn or rebellious behavior

neglect of school work

inability or unwillingness to communicate

promiscuity

use of alcohol or drugs

truancy or running away

neglect of personal appearance

loss of weight

sudden changes in personality
difficulty in concentration

Measures that can be used to prevent adolescent suicides are much the same as those for people of other ages (see Chapter 20). However, since parents and school officials have a great deal of control over adolescents, there are some special precautions which can be taken. Since adolescent suicide attempts are often sudden and impulsive, guns and poison should be kept away from the young potential suicide. Schools and parents should encourage friendships and extracurricular activities. Parents and teachers can also watch closely for the warning signs of depression and suicidal preoccupation.

SUICIDE AMONG BLACKS

As pointed out in the previous section, suicide among young blacks, especially among men, is a serious problem. Whereas suicide rates reach their peak fairly late in life in the population as a whole, blacks in their teens and early twenties have a higher incidence of suicide than do older people of the same ethnic group. Seiden (1970) said that suicide among young blacks has "undergone striking, epidemic increase in the last 15 years."

Hendin (1969) has described the syndrome of "black suicide" as it relates to ghetto family patterns. The absence of a father in the family, which dates back to the days of slavery when black family ties were not respected, seems especially significant. The young black who comes from a family with no resident father may feel a combination of rage against others and despair that he will ever have the love and support of a father. Relations with the mother are also disturbed relative to non-ghetto patterns. Mothers, especially those with illegitimate children, often leave a child to be cared for by its grandmother or aunt while the mother works in another town or goes to live with a man who does not want the child around. The child may later be taken from the foster parent to go once again to live with the biological mother. This treatment seems to lead to rage and despair; rage against the rejecting mother and despair of finding a secure place in her affection. These feelings about the parents may go unresolved and last into adulthood, where they interfere with the achievement of successful marriage. Suicide may be a way of attempting to resolve these conflicts about the parents. It may also be the result of distress and confusion about an inability to form adult relationships that will satisfy the lingering childhood needs.

Seiden (1970) has described other forms of stress that urban blacks encounter when they reach adulthood. First, of course, unemployment comes first to the young black man. In a society where to work is to be worthwhile, the young black is often unable to work. The result of unemployment is emotional as well as financial, ending in feelings of incompetence and torpor. According to Seiden, the effects of job loss may be responsible for the high suicide rate among older whites. Since unemployment hits young blacks hard, their suicide rate shows its effect at an early age.

When job opportunities appear, they may raise the suicide rate among young blacks rather than lower it. After a long period of deprivation and frustration, hopes may rise too fast when a break comes. Expectations may rise far beyond the satisfactions that could realistically be obtained. Frustration at such a point could cause a much more explosive reaction than would have occurred during a period when employment opportunities were very low.

Seiden felt that suicidal behavior among young blacks included a kind of act that is relatively rare among whites: victim-precipitated homicide, in which the victim brings about his own death at the hands of another person. The suicide rate for young blacks would be far higher if statistics included this sort of death. Seiden also suggested (more controversially) that "militant black revolutionaries may be suicidally motivated, and their activities may serve them as a subculturally acceptable alternative to the so-called 'inadvertent' overdose." (1970, p. 24)[1]

Why should young blacks seek death through the violence of others rather than by themselves? Seiden suggested some possible motives. He felt that suicide *per se* is unacceptable in the black ghetto subculture. It is regarded by young black males as an unmasculine thing to do. The young urban black man is expected (and expects himself) to be able to take what life sends him without complaining or breaking down. He also regards violence as an excellent way to solve problems. When suicidal impulses motivate him, he may find that the best solution to his conflicting needs is to create violence which will damage the world and will lead in its turn to his own death. For the young black revolutionary, a further motivation might be the desire for martyrdom as a way to achieve high status.

[1] As support for this idea, Seiden points out that the Black Panthers have continued in provocative behavior in spite of repression, while effective revolutionary groups have tended to go underground under similar circumstances.

SUICIDE AMONG AMERICAN INDIANS

Suicide among a number of American Indian tribes has been at a high level for some years. Dizmang (1967) has described the situation he found when asked to give advice on a near-epidemic of suicide among adolescents of the Northern Cheyenne.

The Cheyenne, when they were a free and well-functioning group, had their own culturally prescribed ways of dealing with self-esteem and aggression. Suicide was rare among men in the earlier days of the tribe. When a man was distressed by loss of esteem, he organized a small war party to raid some enemy tribe. He would either regain his self-esteem through some brave act during the fight, or die in the attempt. The Cheyenne women were more likely to kill themselves, usually by hanging, particularly if their marriages were unhappy or childless. Even among the women, though, suicide was fairly rare.

A form of suicide-like behavior was prevalent among the men. It was the Sun Dance ritual, in which the dancer thrust sharpened sticks through his pectoral muscles. The sticks were tied to a pole, and the individual danced backward, staring at the sun, sometimes until the sticks tore their way out of his muscles. This ritual, according to Dizmang, was "as important in handling aggressive feelings as going into battle with an enemy."

When the Cheyenne were placed on the reservation, these ways of handling aggression were forbidden. Since the buffalo had become nearly extinct, buffalo hunting, another way of expressing aggression, was almost impossible. As their time-honored means of dealing with aggression were removed, factors which decreased self-esteem were brought in. The Cheyenne men were required to cut their long hair, which had been valued highly as a symbol of strength. Since the loss of the old way of life had made it impossible for the Indians to support themselves on the reservation, welfare programs were brought in, further undercutting self-esteem.

Dizmang attributed the high suicide rate among the Cheyenne to a loss of the old ways of handling aggression or loss of face as well as to the lack of self-esteem inherent in the reservation life. The individual becomes "boxed in" between his own basic needs and the impossibility of gratification in his environment. Escape is the only means of dealing with the situation. It can come through alcohol, severe depression, or violent involvement with homicide, suicide, or accidents.

One solution for the Cheyenne would be to leave the reservation and to join the white man's culture. However, one of the highest Cheyenne values is loyalty to the tribe, which would be violated by leaving. In addition, there are no small Cheyenne communities off the reservation that could help the "emigrant" in his transition. Between the guilt about leaving the reservation and the fact that he must make a precipitous change, joining the white culture becomes less and less of a viable alternative for the Cheyenne. The real alternative seems to be the improvement of the reservation culture. As Dizmang said,

> The larger problem is basically one of "community organization" in a broad sense. These terribly "beaten" people still hold onto a core of pride and self-respect. They are still basically an industrious and intelligent people. If these latent but dying internal resources could be tapped, a cultural process of self-renewal rather than self-destruction could be reinstated (1967, p. 11).

CONCLUSION

Some subgroups which have particularly serious suicide problems differ from the population as a whole. Young people, among whom suicide is a leading cause of death, are more likely to complete suicide if they are married than if they are single. Suicide in adolescents seems related most often to problems of controlling sexual impulses and achieving sexual identity, and to the maintenance of self-esteem in the face of scholastic pressure. Suicide among blacks is at a peak during youth rather than old age, a situation opposite to that seen among whites. Unemployment and the effect of family relationships seem important here. Victim-precipitated homicide is also common in this group. American Indians on reservations sometimes show suicide rates of near-epidemic proportions. The problem has been blamed on a breakdown in cultural ways of dealing with aggression and loss of self-esteem.

BIBLIOGRAPHY

BALSER, B. H., and MASTERSON, J. F. 1959. Suicide in adolescents. *Amer. J. Psychiat.* 116: 400–404.

DIZMANG, L. H. 1967. Suicide among the Cheyenne Indians. *Bull. Suicidol.* July: 8–11.

HENDIN, H. 1969. *Black Suicide*. New York: Basic Books Inc., Publishers.

LYMAN, J. L. 1961. Student suicide at Oxford University. *Student Med.* 10 (2): 260–64.

McCLELLAND, D. 1963. The Harlequin complex. In R. W. White, ed. *The Study of Lives.* New York: Atherton Press.

MINTZ, R. S. 1964. A pilot study of the prevalence of persons in the city of Los Angeles who have attempted suicide. Upubl. ms., UCLA Neuropsychiatric Institute, Los Angeles.

MUNTER, P. K. 1966. Depression and suicide in college students. In L. McNeer, ed. *Proceedings of Conference on Depression and Suicide in Adolescents and Young Adults,* Fairlee, Vt.: Vermont Dept. of Mental Health, pp. 20–25.

SCHMID, C. F., and VAN ARSDOL, M. D. 1955. Completed and attempted suicides. *Amer. Sociol. Rev.* 20: 273–83.

SEIDEN, R. H. 1966. Campus tragedy: a study of student suicide. *J. Abnorm. Psychol.* 71: 389–99.

———— 1969. *Suicide among youth.* U.S. Government Printing Office, Public Health Service, Publication No. 1971.

———— 1970. We're driving young blacks to suicide. *Psychol. Today* 4 (3): 24–28.

STEARNS, A. W. 1953. Cases of probable suicide in young persons without obvious motivation. *J. Maine Med. Assoc.* 44: 16–23.

CHAPTER 14

SOCIOLOGICAL FACTORS IN SUICIDE

In the course of this book, we have spent much time on intrapersonal and interpersonal correlates of suicide. We must also look at some of the external circumstances that may lead to internal changes in the direction of suicide. In Chapter 12, we looked at the effects of sex differences. Sex, like other non-psychological factors, is not itself a cause of suicide, but in combination with other factors may produce a psychological state that can lead to suicide. In this chapter, we will examine a number of other external circumstances which, like sex, do not directly produce suicide, but which may contribute to the development of suicidal tendencies. In the case of each of these variables, the interaction that leads to suicide is very complex. Thus, we cannot use demographic factors to make predictions about the suicidal tendencies of any one person. However, when we look at large groups of people, we may find differences in suicide rates that seem dependent upon some external factor, such as social class.

In discussing demographic variables, we will look at them in terms of three different categories: 1. Static variables: circumstances that do not change over some period of time. Place of residence would be an example of a static variable. 2. Dynamic environmental variables: changes that are taking place in the world, such as war. 3. Dynamic personal variables: changes in the individual relative to the world, such as alterations in social status.

STATIC VARIABLES

PLACE OF RESIDENCE

Most of the older studies have found that the urban suicide rate was higher than the rural rate. More recently, studies have been finding higher rates of suicide in rural areas.

When the rural suicide rate is low, its level is usually attributed to the greater stability of the rural family, the larger number of children, and the unified interests and traditions of rural families. The modern trend to higher suicide rates in rural areas is seen as a result of the increasing social isolation of country life, as well as the disruption of traditional rural life by urban values.

Research by Shneidman and Farberow (1960) examined differences in suicidal behavior in different residential areas of Los Angeles County. They divided the county into one hundred sub-areas, which they classified into three socioeconomic statuses and three types of communities. They then examined the suicide notes written in each type of community and found a number of differences.

In the most advantaged suburbs, the suicide notes stressed reasons for the suicide rather than emotion. The most common reason was *ennui*. People from the most advantaged apartment house areas stressed ill health as the reason for the suicide; the emotional tone was one of guilt, and they asked forgiveness for their act. An example of the emotionless sort of note left in the advantaged suburbs is:

No funeral. Please leave the body to science. William Smith. (Shneidman and Farberow, p. 283)

In the advantaged apartment house areas, the notes were more likely to resemble this:

To all my friends:
Please forgive me and thanks for all your kindness.
My courage has run out. In the face of poor health, deserted by my sisters, and persistent cruelty of my husband I have no further reason to keep fighting.
All my life I have tried to be decent. I have worked hard to make a marriage out of puny material. To be deserted at such a time of my life is more than I can bear. . . . (Shneidman and Farberow, p. 284)

In moderately advantaged suburbs, the motivational pattern as seen in suicide notes rarely expressed guilt or fears about poor health. Conflicts between love and hate were most commonly expressed. Here is a typical note from such an area:

> Mary:
>   Here is the note you wanted, giving you power of attorney for the house and everything else (including all your bills).
>   I hope that my insurance will get you out of the whole mess that you got us both in.
>   This isn't hard for me to do because it's probably the only way I'll ever get rid of you, we both know how the California courts see only the women's side. . . .
>   I think that Junior and Betty and George are really the only things in the world that I'll miss. Please take good care of them.
>   Good luck, Bill . . .
>
> (Shneidman and Farberow, p. 285)

In the moderately advantaged "little cities" of Los Angeles County, suicide notes contained few expressions of affection toward the recipient. Instead, there was anger and a feeling of having been rejected. The least advantaged industrial areas yielded notes which were matter-of-fact instructions about disposal of the body and material possessions.

AGE

Our mythology about suicide regards self-destruction as a problem of the adolescent years. Literary representations of suicide, such as Goethe's young Werther, have strengthened this misconception. In actuality, the rate of completed suicide rises with age, at least in the white population of the United States. The rate for white males continues to rise throughout the life span. The rate for females reaches a peak somewhere between forty-five and sixty-five years of age. (The peak seems to be occurring at an earlier age nowadays than was formerly the case.) Nonwhite males and females show a closer resemblance to young Werther and have their highest suicide rate between ages twenty-five and thirty-four.

In very young people, suicide is rare.[1] Up to the age of fifteen, the rate of completed suicide is less than 0.2 per 100,000 per year. Acts of self-injury are much more common, but they tend to be of such a nature that the probability of death from them is low. The low suicide rate in the very young can be attributed to a number of factors. The concept of

---

[1] One must realize, however, that coroners are almost never willing to label the death of a child less than ten years of age as suicide. The rate of suicide among the very young is probably somewhat higher than it appears to be.

death is probably not well-developed in children and young adolescents, so they would be less likely to choose death as a means of escape. The young also have physical limitations and a lack of knowledge about how to kill themselves. In addition, there may be less precipitating stress, since the youngster is not likely to meet problems as serious as those he will face later on. Clearly, childhood can involve many frustrations, but they do not usually include job loss, social status difficulties, or the fear of serious illness. When a child does commit a self-destructive act, the intent is usually to manipulate other people rather than to die.

When we compare the suicidal behavior of older people with that of young adults, we find many differences. The younger people are more likely to attempt suicide than the older group. Even when older people attempt suicide, their methods are more lethal (likely to cause death) than those of the younger attempters. The motives of older suicidal people have been investigated by looking at their suicide notes (Farberow and Shneidman, 1957). The notes were classified into three categories: those in which suicide was motivated by guilt and the need for punishment, those in which the motivation was the desire to hurt someone else, and those in which the person wanted to escape from something unpleasant in life. With increasing age of the suicidal individual, there was less and less motivation for self-punishment or revenge, and more evidence of a wish to escape discomfort.

Younger adults often have their suicide precipitated by some interpersonal problem. This is less likely with older suicidal individuals. For the latter, the most frequent disturbing event is a serious medical or surgical illness. Other stressful factors may include the death of friends, change of residence, and job or financial problems.

It seems that suicide is most common at ages related to biological or social change, such as the menopause or retirement. According to Sainsbury (1968) this is not the case in societies where elderly people are valued and respected, such as Western Nigeria and prerevolutionary China. Presumably, a positive evaluation of old age helps people withstand the stresses of change.

SOCIETAL ATTITUDE TOWARD SUICIDE

Societies differ markedly in their approval or disapproval of suicidal behavior. Several suicidologists have suggested that the attitude of the society may make a difference to the suicide rate (Dublin and Bunzel, 1933; Farber, 1968). The attitude of the group may account for the low suicide rate among Catholics and the differences in rate among the Scandinavian countries (see Chapter 4).

EMPLOYMENT AS A CORRELATE
OF SUICIDE

In the United States, in recent years, there has been a strong positive correlation between the proportion of unemployed people and the suicide rate for white males. That is, the more people were unemployed at a time, the higher was the suicide rate. Presumably, this relationship stems from the stress of job loss, or fear of loss. (In Chapter 9, the importance of job loss in precipitation of men's suicides was discussed.)

In an analysis of the principal labor market areas of Pennsylvania (Walbran et al., 1965; Lester, 1970a), a somewhat different picture of the relationship appeared. There was a negative correlation between the proportion of unemployment and the incidence of completed suicide over the labor market areas; that is, areas with low unemployment had high suicide rates, and vice versa. Perhaps (as H. Wechsler commented in a personal communication) an explanation of these results is the "fit" hypothesis: people with a particular characteristic who live in communities where the characteristic is less common should have a higher incidence of emotional disturbance than if they lived in communities where their characteristic was common.

OCCUPATIONAL STATUS AND
OCCUPATION

In general, the suicide rate seems to be highest among members of the highest status occupational groups. This is not to say that suicide is no problem in the middle and lower status groups; there is simply a tendency for increase in the rate along with an increase in occupational status. The relationship may actually be even stronger than is apparent. The suicides of upper status individuals are much more likely to be disguised and kept out of official statistics than are those of low status people. Upper status families may have the death dealt with by a private physician, while the low status suicide may be taken to the emergency room of a public hospital.

It appears that even if we keep status constant, people in certain occupations commit suicide more frequently than others. It has been suggested (Farber, 1968) that those whose profession involves giving nurturance and help to others have an increased suicide rate. Of all types of physicians, for example, the group with the highest suicide rate is psychiatrists, who in some ways are faced with the greatest demand for interpersonal giving. The suicide rates of service workers (policemen, barbers, nurses, etc.) also seem to be higher than those of craftsmen (carpenters, tailors, etc.).

DYNAMIC ENVIRONMENTAL VARIABLES

THE ECONOMY

Jokes, cartoons, and anecdotes have fostered the idea of a high suicide rate (especially among upper class males) following the stock market crash of 1929. It is true that there was a rise in the male completed suicide rate during the economic depression, but the high rate was not associated with any particular dramatic event. It seems to have been related only to the general state of the economy.

When the relationship of suicide to the state of the economy was investigated by Henry and Short (1954), it appeared that the influence of the economy acted as a dynamic rather than as a static variable. That is, the depressed state of the economy alone does not necessarily increase the suicide rate. Rather, it is a *change* in the economy that seems to affect the incidence of suicidal behavior. In particular, as one might expect, the rate of suicide increases during periods of business contraction.

THE EFFECTS OF WAR

Emotionally speaking, war has many effects on people other than its role as a means of settling international disputes. It may free some individuals to act out aggressive fantasies and allow others a moratorium on career decisions. For some men, it may be a shattering event such that all the rest of their lives are spent trying to resolve the feelings engendered by the war. For some women, it means a chance to break away from social constraints by getting out of the home; for others, it may be a time of unending anxiety; for still others, it may be an opportunity for promiscuity without guilt. With all these psychodynamic functions of war, one would predict correctly that suicide rates would change during the years of international conflict.

In general, it appears that the suicide rate for men decreases during wartime. The rate for women seems to depend on the time and place; it was unaffected in the U.S. during World II, whereas the rate for married women increased in Paris during World War II.

A number of theories have been proposed to explain the wartime change in suicide rate. (These have been discussed in detail by Rojcewicz,

1969.) One suggestion is that the male rate falls because suicide-prone people can act out their impulses and die in battle without having their deaths recorded as suicide. However, it appears that the male suicide rate falls for all age groups, not just for those in active service.

A second explanation comes from the idea that suicide is aggression turned against the self (for a detailed discussion, see Chapter 7). War makes outward-directed aggression legitimate. Since the increase in outward aggression should lower the level of aggressiveness, there should be a reduction in the need to attack the self. However, the drop in suicide rates seems to have occurred mainly during the great international wars and not during dynastic struggles. The suicide rate also drops in neutral countries during wars.

If this second explanation is valid, it suggests that there should be low suicide rates among people whose occupations allow them to be aggressive. This is not true for the peacetime military, but may be true of policemen who are permitted to be brutally aggressive. According to Friedman (1967), when New York City police were restrained from brutality, following Tammany Hall's fall from power in 1934, their suicide rate rose drastically.

Another hypothesis about the wartime suicide rate is that suggested by the sociologist Emile Durkheim. Durkheim proposed that during war the social integration of a society increases, and, as a result, the likelihood of suicide is decreased. This idea is supported by the decrease in suicide in France during the Occupation, when people's greatest concern was solidarity in their resistance to the Germans. Suicide rates were apparently low in the concentration camps, where individuality was attacked and the group emphasized. The decrease in suicide rate of the military during wartime could also result from increased social integration as groups of soldiers become unified during combat.

COMMUNITY GROWTH

A changing community can lead to personal disturbance for many community members. People may find that the neighborhoods in which they have lived for many years drastically change character. A family may find itself socially "isolated" among families of different ethnic background or social class. Older people may find that the landmarks of their childhood disappear, leaving them in a city that seems foreign to them.

In a study of fifty communities near Boston (Wechsler, 1961), it was found that the towns that were growing rapidly had high rates of depressive disorders and suicide. Similarly, it appears (according to Quinney, 1965) that, in countries where urbanization or industrialization are increasing quickly, the suicide rate is relatively high, while the homicide rate is relatively low.

In order to explain the suicide rate differences in the communities, we can examine two theories. One suggestion is that population growth leads to social conditions that increase the likelihood of suicide; this idea will be discussed below in the section on social disorganization. The second hypothesis states that suicidal individuals drift or migrate into areas that are undergoing population change. This seems more likely to be true for towns within a country than for different nations. The drift hypothesis will be discussed later in this chapter.

SOCIAL DISORGANIZATION

The term social disorganization refers to many factors within a community, such as overcrowding, the infant mortality rate, and the incidence of juvenile delinquency. Such disorganization may come about as a result of rapid population change, of loss of employment, or of other variables.

The precise relation of suicide rate to criteria of social disorganization seems to depend on the area being studied. In Scotland, rates of both attempted and completed suicide were high in areas that were over-crowded and that had a high rate of juvenile delinquency. The divorce rate and the incidence of reports of cruelty to children were also high. There was no apparent association between a high suicide rate and incidence of infant mortality, eviction notices, rent arrears, or peace warnings (Philip and McCulloch, 1966; McCulloch et al., 1967).

In Buffalo, N.Y., a very different picture was found (Lester, 1970b). There were no relationships between the rate of completed suicide and overcrowding or incidence of crime among young people. The completed suicide rate was high where there was a high percentage of elderly people, of college educated people, and of widowed and divorced people.

In Santiago, Chile, there was still a different pattern (Chuaqui et al., 1966). The incidence of completed suicide correlated positively with population density and negatively with infant mortality. That is, suicide was frequent where the population was highly crowded, but infrequent where infant mortality was high. (This seems somewhat contradictory because infant mortality is usually highest in the most overcrowded parts of a city.)

Again, a study of suicide in London from 1929 to 1933 gave a different set of results (Sainsbury, 1955). Overcrowding seemed to have no influence on the suicide rate. Where poverty was frequent, the suicide rate was low; where there was a large percentage of middle class individuals, it was high. A high incidence of completed suicide was found in areas where many people lived alone, where there were many immigrants, and where the divorce and illegitimacy rates were high. The incidence of juvenile delinquency did not seem related to the suicide rate. Obviously, the data from these studies are in conflict. Completed suicide did not correlate with infant mortality in Edinburgh, but they were negatively related in Santiago. Overcrowding correlated with the suicide rate in Edinburgh and Santiago, but not in London and Buffalo. These inconsistencies could mean that the relationships between the suicide rate and the factors we have listed are too weak to be useful for an understanding of suicide. Or, they could mean that suicidal behavior is determined differently in London, Edinburgh, Santiago, and Buffalo. This could well be the case, since cross-cultural studies seem to indicate that suicide has different motivations in different cultures. However, it is impossible at the moment to know which alternative is correct.

Perhaps there are too many variables at work for study of social disorganization and suicide in cities to be successful. One study (Kahne, 1968) looked instead at the suicide rate and social disorganization in a psychiatric hospital. There seemed to be an influence of population instability on suicidal behavior. Months in which a patient committed suicide tended to follow periods of high turnover in staff and patient population. When personnel quit their jobs or patients were discharged there was no effect on the incidence of suicides. The influx of new people into the hospital seemed to be the crucial factor. Bringing in new people must have resulted in a temporary social disorganization. This in turn affected some individuals in ways that brought about their suicide.

DYNAMIC PERSONAL VARIABLES

SUICIDE AND MIGRATION

An individual who migrates to a new country or city is bound to find himself having to adapt to the new situation. He may have to live in a house differing from the kind he is used to and he may have to eat strange food. Above all, he will have to make new friends, get used to a new job, and, in general, create for himself a new niche in the social structure. It may take years before he truly feels at home in his new environment. The period of adaptation may be still further extended if the migrant left his homeland against his will and if he clings to his old memories in a desperate attempt to retain his national identity.

The completed suicide rate of immigrants to the United States is greater than that of native-born citizens, and also greater than the rate in the immigrants' home countries (Sainsbury and Barraclough, 1968).

The same thing has been found for immigrants to other places, such as Hong Kong.

Rates of attempted suicide seem about the same for immigrants and the native-born. Why should this be, when the immigrants clearly have a higher completed suicide rate? Perhaps the answer lies in the motivation for the suicidal act. A common motivation for attempted suicide is the desire to manipulate the behavior of other people. The immigrant is much more likely than the native-born to be socially isolated—that is, to have no one close enough to him to manipulate. Therefore, one reason for *attempting* suicide would be missing. As far as the completion of suicide is concerned, the immigrant may have many reasons to wish to escape from an intolerable environment. Perhaps it is also the case that those who immigrate are predisposed to suicide for the sake of escape. They may have left their native country because of a tendency to escape from problems rather than to try to solve them. Suicide may seem to be the only means of escape when the person finds he has run as far as he can and still has his problems with him.

CHANGE OF SOCIAL CLASS

A rise or fall in social status may move an individual into an environment as foreign to him as if he had migrated to another country. (James Baldwin has, in fact, used these last words as the title of a book that describes the cultural differences between Harlem and fashionable Manhattan). Completed suicides have frequently experienced downward social mobility, although upward mobility is found as well (Breed, 1963; Porterfield and Gibbs, 1960). In the case of the upwardly mobile suicides, we might attribute their acts to relative social isolation within their new class. (Such people might also be pushed to suicide by some failure in performance.) It is more difficult to explain the case of the downwardly mobile individual. He too may be socially isolated. On the other hand, it may be that his general inability to cope with the world, which culminates in suicide, is also instrumental in bringing about a fall in social class.

CONCLUSION

Demographic factors, whether static or dynamic, seem to operate on individuals in such a way that the suicide rate is affected. The individual's place of residence is related to his motivation as expressed in a suicide note. Urban areas formerly had a consistently higher incidence of suicide than rural areas, but this difference is no longer clear-cut. Groups of older people show more suicidal behavior than groups of the young; in fact, completed suicide is almost nonexistent among those under fifteen years of age. Occupational status also has an effect, with a higher suicide rate found among the highest status occupations. Business contraction increases the suicide rate, while war decreases the rate among males. Communities that are either growing quickly or socially disorganized have higher suicide rates than more stable areas. Immigrants to a city or country and those who have changed social class also have an increased suicide rate.

BIBLIOGRAPHY

Breed, W. 1963. Occupational mobility and suicide among white males. *Amer. Sociol. Rev.* 28: 178–88.

Chuaqui, C., Lemkau, P. V., Legarreta, A. and Contreras, M. A. 1966. Suicide in Santiago, Chile. *Pub. Hlth. Rep.* 81: 1109–17.

Dublin, L., and Bunzel, B. 1933. *To be or not to be.* New York: Harrison Smith and Robert Haas.

Durkheim, E. 1951. *Suicide.* Glencoe, Ill.: The Free Press.

Farber, M. L. 1968. *Theory of suicide.* New York: Funk & Wagnalls.

Farberow, N. L., and Shneidman, E. S. 1957. Suicide and age. In E. S. Shneidman and N. L. Farberow, eds. *Clues to suicide.* New York: McGraw-Hill Book Company.

Friedman, P. 1967. Suicide among police. In E. S. Shneidman, ed. *Essays in self-destruction.* New York: Science House, p. 414–49.

Henry, A. F., and Short, J. F. 1954. *Suicide and homicide.* Glencoe, Ill.: The Free Press.

Kahne, M. J. 1968. Suicide in mental hospitals. *J. Hlth. Soc. Behav.* 9: 255–66.

Lester, D. 1970a. Suicide and unemployment. *Arch. Environ. Hlth.* 20: 277–78.

——— 1970b. Social disorganization and suicide. *Social Psychiat.* 5: 175–76.

McCulloch, J. W., and Philip, A. E. 1967. Social variables in attempted suicide. *Acta. Psychiat. Scand.* 43: 341–46.

Philip, A. E., and McCulloch, J. W. 1966. Use of social indices in psychiatric epidemiology. *Brit. J. Prev. Soc. Med.* 20: 122–26.

Porterfield, A. L. and Gibbs, J. P. 1960. Occupational prestige and social mobility of suicides in New Zealand. *Amer. J. Sociol.* 66: 147–52.

QUINNEY, R. 1965. Suicide, homicide, and economic development. *Social Forces* 43: 401–6.

ROJCEWICZ, S. J. 1969. Suicide and lethal aggression. Amer. Assn. Suicidol. New York.

SAINSBURY, P. 1955. *Suicide in London.* London: Chapman and Hall, Ltd.

────── 1968. Suicide and depression. In A. Coppen and A. Walk, eds. Recent developments in affective disorders. *Brit. J. Psychiat.* Special publication no. 2: 1–13.

SAINSBURY, P., and BARRACLOUGH, B. 1968. Differences between suicide rates. *Nature* 220: 1252.

SHNEIDMAN, E. S., and FARBEROW, N. L. 1960. A socio-psychological investigation of suicide. In H. P. David and J. C. Brengelman, eds. *Perspectives in personality research.* New York: Springer Publishing Co., Inc., pp. 270–93.

WALBRAN, B., MACMAHON, B., and BAILEY, A. E. 1965. Suicide and unemployment in Pennsylvania, 1954–1961. *Arch. Environ. Hlth.* 10: 11–15.

WECHSLER, H. 1961. Community growth, depressive disorders, and suicide. *Amer. J. Sociol.* 67: 9–16.

CHAPTER 15

SOCIOLOGICAL THEORIES OF SUICIDE

In the previous chapter, we discussed some of the ways in which the suicide rate varies from one group of people to another. Sociologists have tried to develop theories to explain why the frequency of suicide is different in different populations. Up to the present, sociological theories have been concerned solely with completed suicide rather than with suicide attempts or threats.

The attention of sociologists to differences in suicide rate dates back to the French sociologist Emile Durkheim, whose work was done at the turn of the last century. Durkheim attempted to justify the use of a sociological rather than a psychological approach:

> We have in fact shown that for each social group there is a specific tendency to suicide explained neither by the organic-psychic constitution of individuals nor by the nature of the physical environment. Consequently, by elimination, it must necessarily depend upon social causes . . . (Durkheim, 1951, p. 145)

Durkheim had examined psychological factors that might influence suicide rates and found that they had no predictive power. By elimination, then, he decided that sociological variables must have explanatory power. (Durkheim did not seem to consider the possibility that perhaps no variable will be able to explain intergroup differences in suicide rates. And, of course, his ruling out of psychological causes of suicide has not been supported.)

Actually, there is no need to argue in favor of the sociological study of suicide. Differences in groups' suicide rates present a real sociological problem. Suicide rates within a group tend to remain rather stable. This suggests that group suicide rates are reliable and amenable to study.

In this chapter, we will examine some of the most important sociological theories of suicide. For each theory, we will also look at some of the research that has attempted to test predictions derived from that theory.

DURKHEIM'S THEORY

The theory developed by Durkheim is the predecessor of all sociological approaches to suicide. Most of the other theories we will examine are modernizations or reformulations of Durkheim's ideas. However, as the reader will see, part of the continued interest in developing Durkheim's theory stems from the lack of explicit definition of the variables in the original theory.

The basic concepts in Durkheim's analysis involve four etiological types of suicidal behavior. The first pair, egoistic suicide and altruistic suicide, is based on the idea of integration of a societal group. Durkheim himself did not give a very clear definition of what he meant by social integration, but other workers have tried to interpret his idea. A society is integrated to the extent that its members possess shared beliefs and sentiments, an interest in one another, and a common sense of devotion to common goals. Social integration increases when members of the group have more durable and stable social relationships. Suicidal behavior is common in societies where there is a high degree of social integration (altruistic suicide) and in those where there is a low degree of social integration (egoistic suicide). Societies with a moderate degree of social integration have the lowest suicide rate. Egoistic suicide results from excessive individualism, which is prevented by religions with strong group ties, strong family and parental ties, or strong political affiliations. When the social ties in a society are minimal, suicide becomes more likely. At the other extreme of social integration, a person can be too closely identified with a particular group. He may then take his life as a religious sacrifice or as the result of political or military allegiances.

The second group of two types of suicidal motivation was based on the variable of social regulation. A society is regulated to the extent that it controls the emotions and motivations of individual members. Fatalistic suicide is common in societies with a high degree of social regulation, while anomic suicide occurs frequently in societies with a low degree of social regulation. As with social integration, societies with a moderate degree of social regulation have the lowest incidence of suicidal behavior. When the degree of social regulation in a society is low, the individual's

> . . . passions are apt to burst forth, he may become disoriented, and will perhaps kill himself. Anomie occurs among businessmen, especially during booms and depressions, and among widows and divorced people. (Johnson, 1965, p. 876).

At the other extreme of social regulation, people's futures

> . . . become pitilessly blocked and passions violently choked by oppressive discipline. This social cause of suicide occurs among childless married women, very young husbands, and slaves. (Johnson, 1965, p. 876).

As pointed out above, Durkheim's statements were often so unclear as to leave the modern reader very much in the dark about exactly what he meant. There are, for example, two ways of interpreting Durkheim's ideas on the relationship between social behavior, shared sentiments and morals (that is, social meanings), and the occurrence of suicide. One interpretation argues that social behavior is the cause of social meanings and thence of suicide. The chain of events has been described in this way:

1. The morphological factors (the demographic and ecological characteristics of a society) cause certain degrees and certain patterns of social interaction.
2. The degrees and patterns of social interaction then cause a certain degree of "social integration."
3. "Social integration," defined as either states of individuals or as a state of the society, is then defined as the "strength of the individual's ties to society."
4. The "strength of ties" is then defined either in terms of egoism . . . and anomie or else the "strength of ties" is hypothesized to be the cause of the given degrees of egoism . . . and anomie.
5. Egoism is defined as a relative lack of social or collective activity that gives meaning and object to life . . . and anomie is defined as a relative lack of social activity that acts to *constrain* the individual's passions, which, without constraint, increase "infinitely."
6. And finally, the given balance of the degrees of egoism . . . and anomie is hypothesized to be the cause of the given suicide rate of the society. (Douglas, 1967, pp. 39–40)

This interpretation of Durkheim's theory is the one that has most often been accepted by American sociologists. Douglas, whom we quoted above, argued that the interpretation is incorrect. Instead, he suggested that social meanings cause social behavior and thus suicide. Douglas pointed out that Durkheim vacillated between the two positions, but felt that ultimately he had come to the second. In the second interpretation, anomie and egoism are

> . . . orientations toward the (primarily moral) meanings that constitute society. . . . They seem to represent the generalized orientations toward society of submissiveness, aloofness (or superiority), and rebelliousness. (Douglas, 1967, p. 53)

Durkheim never concerned himself about the social meanings present in a given situation. He did not consider the problem of how to detect and understand the meanings. He assumed, in fact, that social meanings are always immediately obvious to the sociologist who is a member of the society he is studying. Thus, Durkheim felt that there was no need to provide empirical support for the conclusions of the sociologist, since the latter must be correct. Unfortunately, social meanings are different for differing sub-groups of a society (for example, specific age groups or religious factions). The sociologist cannot belong to all possible sub-groups, so he is bound to misunderstand the social meanings that are present in some situations. In considering empirical data, Durkheim appears to have supplied whatever social meanings made the data fit the theory.

> Even when he was aware of common-sense interpretations that were completely contrary to his own, he continued to use common-sense interpretations with complete confidence. The only plausible explanation seems to be that he assumed the whole theory to be true, so any particulars must necessarily fit—if only the theorist will look around for the "right" interpretation. (Douglas, 1967, p. 71)

Durkheim's theorizing can be criticized in many ways, although the faults are those of his time more than of the man himself. He interpreted information in ways that would support his theory. His statistical analyses were naive by modern standards. He failed to give clear definitions of his concepts and to provide guidelines for operationalizing the theoretical elements. The theory ended by being so flexible that it was irrefutable. Nonetheless, Durkheim's influence on sociological studies of suicide has been profound. Almost every new contribution by sociologists has attempted to clarify or develop or modify some part of Durkheim's theory.

REFORMULATIONS OF DURKHEIM'S THEORY

JOHNSON'S APPROACH

Johnson (1965) tried to demonstrate that Durkheim's four suicidal types were logically reducible to a single one. First, Johnson felt that the categories of altruistic and fatalistic suicide were dispensable, since almost all of Durkheim's examples of these were pre-modern and poorly documented. In fact, Durkheim himself considered fatalistic suicide to be quite infrequent and unimportant.

More importantly, Johnson attempted to show that egoism and anomie are identical. In Durkheim's analysis, the two states generally occurred together. Durkheim even stated explicitly that anomie and egoism are "usually merely two different aspects of one social state" (Durkheim, 1951, p. 228). If the two variables coincide empirically almost all of the time, it would be redundant to consider them separately. In addition, the two concepts appeared to Johnson to be the same conceptually. Johnson extracted from Durkheim's work three essential features of egoism: lack of interaction among the members of a society, lack of common conscience or goals, and lack of social regulation. The last, of course, is the same as anomie. In several passages, Durkheim himself seemed to regard egoism and anomie as the same. For example, he said,

> When society is strongly integrated, it holds individuals under its control, considers them at its service . . . (Durkheim, 1951, p. 209)

Johnson thus arrived at a simple restatement of Durkheim's complex theory in terms of a single variable:

> The more integrated (regulated) a society, group, or social group is, the lower its suicide rate. (Johnson, 1966, p. 886)

Of course, Johnson's efforts were directed only toward a logical reduction of Durkheim's theory to its basic elements. The neatness of the conclusion is not a substitute for empirical support, nor did Johnson mean it to be.

POWELL'S APPROACH

Powell (1958) proposed a theory of suicide based on a reformulation of Durkheim's concept of anomie. The basic idea was that the incidence of suicide varies with social status—the position held by an individual in an organized social system. The person's goals are set for him by his social status. If he cannot accept these predetermined goals, a condition of anomie results.

> When the ends of action become contradictory, unaccessible or insignificant, a condition of anomie arises. Characterized by a general loss of orientation and accompanied by feelings of "emptiness" and apathy, anomie can be simply conceived as meaninglessness. (Powell, 1958, p. 132)

So far, Powell's theory is much like Durkheim's. However, he departed radically from the older theory by proposing that there are two distinct forms of anomie. Anomie of dissociation, a characteristic of the lower classes, is a dissociation of the self from the culture's conceptual system. The reaction to confronting chaos (the world as seen without a conceptual system) is fear, which results in flight and aggression. On the other hand, anomie of envelopment, which is characteristic of the upper classes, involves the envelopment of the self by the culture. There is a lack of spontaneity, a result of the unexamined commitment to the prevailing conceptual framework. Either form of anomie raises an individual's probability of suicide.

New names do not make a new theory, however. Upon comparing Powell's two forms of anomie with Durkheim's concepts, we may note that anomie of dissociation appears to be the same as Durkheim's idea of anomie, while anomie of envelopment appears identical with Durkheim's idea of fatalism. Thus, Powell's approach did not really take matters any further than Durkheim had gone.

GINSBERG'S REFORMULATION

Ginsberg (1966) reinterpreted the idea of anomie in terms of a psychological rather than a sociological concept. He related anomie to "level of aspiration," the ambitiousness of a person's goals or intentions. In Durkheim's concept, anomie resulted when lack of social restraints allowed a person's desires to grow without control, and to become insatiable.

Ginsberg noted that anomie was considered to arise from the unhappiness or dissatisfaction of individuals. He postulated that anomie was a direct function of dissatisfaction, which was in turn a function of the difference between satisfactions received and aspiration level. In the normal process, there are internalized social norms, dependent on the individual's social position, which regulate changes in his level of aspiration. The level of aspiration thus remains proportional to the rewards, and the individual feels relatively satisfied. In the anomic process, on the other hand, there are no constraints on the level of aspiration, and it runs ahead of the rewards, resulting in unhappiness for the individual.

Ginsberg suggested that appropriate changes in aspiration level occur only if the individual sees the relationship between what he does and the rewards he receives. In other words, in order for aspiration level to be flexible, the individual must have a sense of efficacy, a feeling that he can affect the world. His aspiration level will increase when he comes to believe that, through his own efforts, he can gain higher rewards in the future. It will decrease when he believes rewards will fall in the future.

It is notable that Ginsberg's thinking, like that of Powell and Johnson, dealt only with reformulating Durkheim's concepts. None of these workers have explained exactly why anomie should lead to suicide in particular, rather than simply stating that dissatisfaction and unhappiness may be direct causes.

GIBBS AND MARTIN'S STATUS INTEGRATION THEORY

Gibbs and Martin (1964) felt that Durkheim's theory was inadequate in many ways. They agreed with previous workers that the distinction between anomie and egoism was slight. They also criticized Durkheim for his failure to give operational definitions of social regulation or to correlate any measure of social integration with suicide rates. Gibbs and Martin worked to remedy Durkheim's omission and to develop an improved sociological theory of suicide. Their ideas can be summarized in five postulates. First,

> The suicide rate of a population varies inversely with the stability and durability of social relationships within that population. (Gibbs and Martin, 1964, p. 27)

Since sociological knowledge about social relationships is not advanced enough to allow stability and durability to be tested directly, Gibbs and Martin postulated a second related idea.

> The stability and durability of social relationships within a population vary directly with the extent to which individuals in that population conform to the patterned and socially sanctioned demands and expectations placed upon them by others. (Gibbs and Martin, 1964, p. 27)

The demands and expectations of others make up a person's social role. A person with a particular status has to conform to a certain role if he wants to maintain stable social relationships. However, almost every person has several different statuses simultaneously, so he may come into conflict about how he should act (it is hard, for example, to act like both a father and a son simultaneously). When conformity to one role interferes with conformity to another, the individual has difficulty maintaining his social relationships. This leads to Gibbs and Martin's third postulate:

> The extent to which individuals in a population conform to patterned and socially sanctioned demands and expectations placed upon them by others varies inversely with the extent to which individuals in that population are confronted with role conflicts. (p. 27)

If two statuses with conflicting roles are occupied simultaneously, they are incompatible. This idea is summed up in the fourth postulate:

> The extent to which individuals in a population are confronted with role conflicts varies directly with the extent to which individuals occupy incompatible statuses in that population. (p. 27)

Finally, Gibbs and Martin postulated that

> The extent to which people occupy incompatible statuses in a population varies inversely with the degree of status integration in that population. (p. 27)

These postulates were combined to produce this hypothesis:

> The suicide rate of a population varies inversely with the degree of status integration in that population. (p. 27)

Gibbs and Martin have tested their hypothesis against data on suicide rates in the United States. Their measure of status integration was a simple one, and one open to criticism: the more people that belonged to a certain status category, the more highly integrated it was assumed to be. The results of the comparisons strongly supported Gibbs and Martin's hypothesis. The higher the status integration of a group, the lower the suicide rate, and vice versa.

HENRY AND SHORT'S
FRUSTRATION-AGGRESSION THEORY

One sociological theory of suicide has been founded on basic ideas other than Durkheim's. Henry and Short (1954) based their theory on a psychological concept, the frustration-aggression hypothesis developed by Dollard, et al. (1939). This hypothesis suggests that aggressive behavior does not develop from an internal drive that needs satisfaction (as eating does), but instead is produced when the environment frustrates the individual by blocking his approach to a goal.

Henry and Short predicted that aggressive behaviors would occur in different patterns, depending on the extent to which the environment offered frustration. In particular, they suggested that the business cycle should affect aggressive behavior. It was predicted that, a) suicide rates will rise during times of business depression and fall during times of business prosperity, while crimes of violence against others will rise during business prosperity and fall during business depression, and b) the effect of the business cycle on suicide rates will be greater for high than for low status groups, while the effect of the business cycle on homicide rates will be greater for low than for high status groups.

Henry and Short concluded that empirical data supported all their predictions. When the data are examined closely, it seems that the support is not as great as Henry and Short thought; however, in general, the predictions were confirmed.

Henry and Short attempted to interpret their results in terms of the frustration-aggression hypothesis. In order to do so, they made a number of assumptions. They assumed, of course, that aggression is often a consequence of frustration. Another assumption was that business cycles produce variations in the hierarchical rankings of persons by status. High status persons lose rank relative to low status persons during business contraction, while low status persons lose relative rank during business expansion. It was also assumed that frustrations are generated by failure to maintain a relative position in the status hierarchy. Finally, Henry and Short assumed that suicide occurs mainly in high status groups, and homicide mainly in low status groups.

Making all these assumptions, let us consider what happens to those who lose income during a business contraction. The higher status person has more income to lose, so his fall is greater than that of the low status person. The high status person loses rank relative to the low status person, and the low status person may actually experience a relative gain in rank. Thus, in times of business contraction, frustration is generated in high status individuals. Since they are prone to direct aggression inward, there is a rise in the suicide rate of high status groups.

The reader will undoubtedly think of many questions about Henry and Short's analysis. For example, who are the people most likely to suffer in a brief business contraction? The high status groups may stand to lose more income, but the low status groups are the first to become unemployed in most recessions.

DOUGLAS' APPROACH

Another sociologist, Douglas (1967), rejected the Durkheim-like analysis of suicide. So far, his approach has yielded a set of categories for describing suicide, rather than a genuine theory. Douglas has been very outspoken in his criticisms of the reliability of official statistics on suicide. Since he did not trust the statistics, he rejected the idea of developing a sociological theory based on statistical comparisons. Instead, he advocated attempts to understand the meanings that suicide can have in a society. For example, in our society, suicidal acts are understood to mean that there is something wrong with the person's situation. A suicidal act may also mean, for a specific person, a way to transform the soul from this world to another, or to transform one's image in this world, or to get revenge.

GENERAL COMMENTS

The sociological approach is a useful one in that it gives information about the relationships between social variables and suicide rates. However, the sociological theories as a whole have left themselves open to some criticisms. We feel that a great deal of time has been wastefully spent in trying to clarify Durkheim's theory, while the investment of energy would have been better put into the development of new concepts. There has been some tendency, too, to make the interpretation of data fit the preexisting assumptions. There have been biases of subject matter (for example, studying only completed suicides) that may have militated against formation of a sound theory. The categorization of sub-groups has often been done according to the classes given by official statistics (for example, all whites versus all blacks), which may not make sense in terms of suicide. Finally, most of the sociological theories have been based on the uncritical use of official statistics, which (as we pointed out in a previous chapter) may be sadly unreliable.

CONCLUSION

Sociological theories deal with the differences in suicide rates found in different groups of people. Many modern theories are derived from the original sociological theory of Durkheim, who felt that suicide could occur in four forms:

1. egoistic suicide, where the individual's suicidal tendencies are not inhibited by strong social ties
2. altruistic suicide, where the person is so identified with the group that he sacrifices himself for it in some way
3. fatalistic suicide, where society blocks realization of the person's goals
4. anomic suicide, where the individual is not involved with his group.

Several more recent workers have tried to reformulate Durkheim's ideas and make his theory a testable one. A theory of suicide based on the concept of status integration has been developed by Gibbs and Martin, who considered Durkheim's approach inadequate. Henry and Short proposed a sociological theory of suicide with a different base, the frustration-aggression hypothesis of Dollard. They believed that suicide results from frustration, and they examined the effects on suicidal behavior of frustration generated by economic fluctuation.

BIBLIOGRAPHY

DOLLARD, J., DOOB, L. W., MILLER, N. E., MOWRER, O. H., and SEARS, R. R. 1939. *Frustration and aggression*. New Haven: Yale University Press.

DOUGLAS, J. D. 1967. *The social meanings of suicide*. Princeton: Princeton University Press.

DURKHEIM, E. 1951. *Suicide*. Glencoe, Ill.: The Free Press.

GIBBS, J. P., and MARTIN, W. T. 1964. *Status integration and suicide*. Eugene, Ore.: University of Oregon Press.

GINSBERG, R. B. 1966. Anomie and aspirations. *Diss. Abstr.* 27A: 3945–46.

HENRY, A. F. and SHORT, J. F. 1954. *Suicide and homicide*. Glencoe, Ill.: The Free Press.

JOHNSON, B. D. 1965. Durkheim's one cause of suicide. *Amer. Sociol. Rev.* 30: 875–86.

POWELL, E. H. 1958. Occupation status and suicide. *Amer. J. Sociol.* 23: 131–39.

CHAPTER 16

DRUGS, ALCOHOL, AND SUICIDAL BEHAVIOR

Alcohol has long been used in Western society in ways that are related to emotional disturbance. In some ways, alcohol can provide benefits which are similar to those of suicidal behavior, but which have the advantage of being reversible. An alcoholic stupor allows the drinker to achieve a temporary escape from the pressing problems of life. Consumption of alcohol may also give the drinker a period of time when he may express hostility as freely as he likes; the folkways decree that insults or attacks committed while drinking should not later be held against a man by his friends. Alcohol may, in addition, be a way of punishing oneself. Too much drinking can result in the loss of friends, job, family, and self-esteem. Clearly, there are some parallels between excessive drinking and suicidal behavior.

The use of drugs in our culture has, until recent years, been very different from the use of alcohol. Drugs have always played a large part in suicidal behavior, since they are relatively simple lethal instruments. However, since it has been only recently that large numbers of people have begun to use drugs for deliberate mood change (as alcohol has been used), we have little information about the functions that drug use serves for individuals. The parallels with suicidal behavior are unclear. As the use of psychoactive drugs becomes more popular, questions are being raised about their relation to suicide. In the popular press, the easy solution to this problem is generally given—that is, that drugs like LSD can directly cause suicide. For example, not long ago, the daughter of a popular entertainer killed herself. She was said to have taken LSD some months prior to her suicide. Since the girl's death, her father has worked hard at warning young people to stay away from the drugs that he feels killed his daughter. This simplistic analysis, which attributes the suicide directly to drug consumption, in this case ignored a whole history of disturbed behavior, including a very early and unhappy marriage.

In this chapter, we will examine the research about the effects of drugs and alcohol on suicidal behavior. As has been our practice in this book, we will not draw conclusions from single, incompletely reported cases like the one mentioned above, but instead will look at evidence gathered from large groups of suicidal people.

DRUGS AS AN INSTRUMENT OF SUICIDE

Drugs are frequently used for committing suicide. In the United States in 1963, analgesics and sleeping pills were the third most popular method for suicide (after firearms and hanging). Of the deaths due to pain-killers and sleeping pills, seventy-five percent were attributed to barbiturates. Tranquilizers were rarely used, although they are prescribed in greater quantity than barbiturates. Tranquilizers are less toxic than barbiturates, and may also produce emotional effects such that the person does not feel like completing the suicide.

DRUGS THAT INDUCE SUICIDE

It has been claimed occasionally that particular drugs make patients depressed and, hence, suicidal. This suggestion has been made for *Rauwolfia serpentina,* which is refined to make a drug used in the treatment of high blood pressure and anxiety. According to Berger (1967), *Rauwolfia* alkaloids are more likely to produce depression and consequent suicide than similar drugs. We must ask, however, whether the drug actually creates depression in a completely normal person, or whether it interacts with previous depressive tendencies and exacerbates them. Similarly, we could raise the question whether patients might be gaining some psychological benefit from their physical and emotional disturbances (for example, self-punishment and relief of guilt). If the disturbances and the psychological benefit were relieved by drug therapy, depression and suicide might take the place of the earlier syndrome.

Another drug, the tranquilizer diazepam (trade name Vallium), has been suspected of inducing suicidal behavior. However, the only satisfactory research on the drug (Gundland, et al., 1966) seems to show no significant differences in suicidal behavior between a control group and diazepam-treated patients.

As we mentioned at the beginning of the chapter, LSD has been implicated as a possible agent leading to suicidal behavior. Cases of attempted and completed suicide have been reported in patients during and after LSD therapy for emotional disturbance. One review of published reports on the topic concluded that

> . . . suicide attempts are an important complication of LSD administration. About one-third of them occurred in persons who took LSD in non-medical settings although seven successful and 12 unsuccessful suicides have occurred as a result of therapy. There is, of course, difficulty in attributing all of these suicides to LSD therapy, as it is typically given to disturbed persons already prone to suicide. Probably no more than half of the suicides would be directly attributed to LSD by the therapists involved. (Smart and Bateman, 1967, p. 6)

We must point out that none of the studies from which the quoted conclusion was drawn was adequately controlled. That is, none of the studies examined the suicide rate of patients of the same sexes, ages, degrees of disturbance, and so on, as those in the LSD therapy group to see whether there was actually a higher incidence of suicide in the LSD group than in similar patients who were not on drug therapy. As for the attribution of the suicides directly to LSD by the therapists involved, we may suggest that therapists, being human, feel distress over their patients' suicides and would prefer to feel that they are not responsible.

When LSD is given for experimental purposes, its effect seems to depend more on the experimenters than on the dose; the same is probably true for the effect of LSD therapy. In some experimental groups, LSD consumption leads to vivid, emotionally-charged moods and hallucinations. In others, the result is a slight feeling of light-headedness and difficulty in fast thinking. Clearly, the effect of the drug varies with the expectations of the people using it. This statement is true not only for laboratory investigations, but also for use of LSD by private individuals. Especially within the youthful "drug culture," interpretation may be crucial to the subjective drug-induced state. One of the authors was told by a student that he, the student, was experiencing "massive hallucinations" during their conversation. Further inquiry revealed that this term meant to the student that when he looked at the office furniture out of the corner of his eye, it made him feel a slightly different mood than it usually did. If a person with some suicidal tendencies expected suicidal behavior to accompany LSD-induced hallucinations, very slight changes in mood might lead him to feel that suicidal behavior was appropriate.

Again, the expectations of the "drug culture" seem to prompt LSD users to classify all unusual perceptions (for example, quite normal negative after-images) as bizarre or crazy. If a user of LSD has never noticed after-images or other ordinary perceptual phenomena before, his first awareness of them may terrify him because he thinks he is having a "bad trip." This sort of thing could also lead to suicide in a person who had already been suicidally inclined.

Some other suggestions have been made with reference to the ways LSD could cause suicide (Cohen, 1968). It could be that LSD produces a presuicidal state of mind: depression, rigidity of thought, and so on. Or, possibly, after one has become "high" on LSD, ordinary life seems empty and meaningless. The descent into reality could then precipitate suicide. A third possibility is that death results accidentally because cognitive distortions hinder the person's reaction to danger (for example, an on-coming car). Finally, some individuals may die as a result of their illusory feelings of power and omnipotence under LSD—while trying to fly like a bird, for example.

If LSD is indeed responsible for suicides that would not otherwise have occurred, it is clear that the mechanism involved is not a simple one. That is, LSD does not punch a magic suicide button in people's heads. In most cases, the drug's effects probably interact with some preexisting suicidal tendency.

Marijuana has rarely been suspected of producing any mood change except mild euphoria. Recently, however, there have been a few reports of unpleasant feelings resulting from marijuana use. Very rarely, users may feel panic and extreme fear. There have been reports of psychotic symptoms following overuse of marijuana (Keup, 1970). Such effects could lead to suicide, but there seem to be no reports relating marijuana use to suicidal behavior.

Some powerful drugs that are in increasing use because of their psychoactive effects may lead into a cycle which may culminate in suicide. For example, the concurrent use of amphetamines and barbiturates may cause extreme emotional disruption. The exciting high produced by amphetamines is followed by a very unpleasant depression. The drug user may take barbiturates to counteract his depressed feeling. In addition, amphetamines stimulate the user to such an extent that he is unable to sleep. Barbiturates may then be taken to induce sleep, and, later, there may be another dose of amphetamines to wake the person up. One of the dangers inherent in this cycle is due to the suppression of dreaming by barbiturates. Experimental evidence shows that a person who is prevented from dreaming becomes irritable and moody. If deprivation goes on long enough, the individual may begin to have waking dreams—that is, hallucinations. These psychological changes can presumably lead to suicide in a person who has suicidal tendencies. The chances that death will occur following amphetamine-barbiturate use are increased by the fact that the development of tolerance for barbiturates does not raise the lethal dosage much for the user (Feldman, 1970). That is, a user may become tolerant of the effect of barbiturates to such an extent that he takes a fatal overdose in his attempt to induce sleep.

DRUG AUTOMATISM

It is sometimes suggested that suicide through a drug overdose can occur without the individual knowing what he is doing. After taking some sleeping pills, the person may be in a partly conscious state. He then may take more pills to achieve sleep, or simply take more pills automatically, with no awareness of the potentially lethal nature of what he is doing. This hypothetical state of partial consciousness has been called "automatism." The idea of drug automatism has been used to explain many deaths through drug overdosage, notably those of Marilyn Monroe and Judy Garland.

In one study of apparent suicides by drugs (Litman et al., 1963), there was no evidence that drug automatism played a part in any of the deaths. In another investigation of ninety-four people who came close to death from drug overdose (Aitken and Proudfoot, 1969), nineteen of the patients claimed that the overdose had been taken during an episode of drug automatism. However, after interviewing the people, the researchers felt that only two of the cases could conceivably have been due to automatism. Some of the patients completely denied having ingested drugs; these people tended to be older, to have used barbiturates more often, and to have gone into deeper comas than those who admitted taking drugs.

Perhaps the assumption that drug automatism *can* occur stems from the belief that suicide is a deliberate, voluntary act, which will always be remembered and admitted. We must, however, realize that a patient may lie about a suicide attempt. He may feel that if he admits his attempt he will be ridiculed, scorned, or incarcerated. If he does not lie, it may well be the case that the attempter actually does not remember his act. Amnesia for the suicidal act can result from two causes. First, a physical trauma can easily result in retrograde amnesia—total loss of memory for a period preceding the injury. This effect characteristically follows accidents in which a person receives a severe blow to the head. It can also result from ingestion of barbiturates or alcohol and from hanging (Stromgren, 1946). Second, amnesia may develop for psychological rather than physiological reasons. The memory of the suicidal act, and of the desperate mood associated with it, may be so distressing to the individual that they are repressed and cannot voluntarily be recalled to memory. In such a case, the person is not lying, but honestly cannot remember what happened. But whether failure to report deliberate drug ingestion is due to lying, somatogenic amnesia, or psychogenic amnesia, the lack of report is by no means clearly attributable to drug automatism.

ALCOHOL CONSUMPTION PRIOR
TO SUICIDE

Alcohol could be involved in a number of ways with suicidal behavior. It could be used in order to ease fear of death and give the individual the courage to kill himself. It could be taken together with barbiturates as a lethal agent. Alternatively, a person who had been drinking without serious suicidal intention might impulsively kill himself while intoxicated.

The proportion of people who drink prior to a suicidal act seems to vary from culture to culture. In England, twenty percent of a sample of attempted suicides have been found to have a high blood alcohol level (Batchelor, 1954), while in the United States, twenty-four percent of male and eleven percent of female completed suicides in another sample had a high blood alcohol level (Shneidman and Farberow, 1961). A study in Yugoslavia (Zmuc, 1968) found a much higher proportion of intoxicated individuals in a sample of completed suicides: sixty percent of the males and thirty-two percent of the females. It is difficult to compare these figures to the number of intoxicated people in the non-suicidal population, but one doubts that, on an ordinary evening in Yugoslavia, sixty percent of the non-suicidal men get drunk. The figures suggest that drinking is found in conjunction with suicidal behavior, although, of course, there is no implication that drinking causes suicide.

ALCOHOLISM AND SUICIDE

Alcoholism, genuine physical and psychological addiction to alcohol, was considered by Karl Menninger (1938) to be a form of suicidal behavior. The alcoholic way of life is clearly destructive to the self and to whatever friends and family remain attached to the alcoholic. Real physiological damage can occur to the liver and brain. Jobs and social relationships are often destroyed, leaving the alcoholic with only the companionship of other heavy drinkers. This self-destructive pattern leads us to ask whether suicidal behavior *per se* is common among alcoholics. Many investigators have estimated that the rates of both completed and attempted suicides are high for alcoholics (from seven to twenty-one percent for attempts, thirteen to forty-six percent for completions).

One hypothesis about the relationship between suicide and alcoholism is that alcoholics have a reduced interest in maintaining their bodily integrity (Stenback and Blumenthal, 1964). That is, alcoholics should be unconcerned about physiological damage done by alcohol or about the pain and mutilation associated with suicidal acts. They should also have a low incidence of hypochondria (pathological fear of illness and concern with bodily functions). Research seems to indicate that the latter, at least, is true; suicidal patients do seem to have a low rate of hypochondria.

Another idea associated with a reduced concern with the body has to do with the general effect of alcohol (Petrie, 1967). It has been suggested that alcohol serves to depress the responsiveness of the body to external stimulation. Under the influence of alcohol, people are less sensitive to pain and more sensitive to boredom or isolation. Lack of stimulation, as in the latter two cases, is even more difficult to bear than usual. A chronic alcoholic might be insensitive to the pain of a suicidal act, and he might have an unusually high tendency toward suicide because of the stress of insufficient social stimulation.

Other researchers (for example, Rushing, 1969) have argued that suicide and alcoholism may be associated because of changes in interpersonal relations. Excessive drinking often causes breaks in family and social ties. The disruption of social relations could lead to isolation, depression, and, finally, suicide.

CONCLUSION

The use of alcohol and drugs is often associated with attempts to change unpleasant moods. By implication, they may also be involved in suicidal behavior. Drugs, especially barbiturates, are popular suicidal methods. Some drugs, notably *Rauwolfia* alkaloids, diazepam, and LSD, have been suspected of causing suicide, but there is no evidence that the suspicion is well-founded. Suicide has also been attributed to "drug automatism," a semi-conscious state in which a lethal overdose is taken. However, there is no evidence that such a state exists. There is more evidence that alcohol is associated with suicide, although not necessarily causally. Drinking precedes a fair proportion of suicidal acts, and the suicide rate among alcoholics is high.

BIBLIOGRAPHY

AITKEN, R. C., and PROUDFOOT, A. T. 1969. Barbiturate automatism. *Postgrad. Med.* 45: 612–16.

BATCHELOR, I. R. C. 1954. Alcoholism and attempted suicide. *J. Ment. Sci.* 100: 451–61.

BERGER, F. M. 1967. The role of drugs in suicide. In L. Yochelson, ed. *Symposium on suicide.* Washington, D. C.: George Washington University, pp. 117–30.

COHEN, S. 1968. The psychedelic way of death. In N. L. Farberow, ed. *Proc. 4th Int. Conf. for Suicide Prevention.* Los Angeles: Delmar, pp. 75–76.

FELDMAN, H. S. 1970. The pill head menace. *Psychosomatics* 11: 99–103.

GUNDLAND, R., ENGELHARDT, D. M., HANKOFF, L., PALEY, H., RUDORFER, L., and BIRD E. 1966. A double-blind outpatient study of diazepam (Valium) and placebo. *Psychopharmacol.* 9: 81–92.

KEUP, W. 1970. Psychotic symptoms due to cannabis abuse. *Dis. Nerv. Syst.* 31: 119–26.

LITMAN, R. E., SHNEIDMAN, E. S., FARBEROW, N. L., TABACHNICK, N., and CURPHEY, T. J. 1963. Investigations of equivocal suicides. *J. Amer. Med. Ass.* 184: 924–29.

MENNINGER, K. 1938. *Man against himself.* New York: Harcourt Brace Jovanovich, Inc.

PETRIE, A. 1967. *Individuality in pain and suffering.* Chicago: The University of Chicago Press.

RUSHING, W. A. 1969. Deviance, interpersonal relations, and suicide. *Hum. Rel.* 22: 61–76.

SHNEIDMAN, E. S., and FARBEROW, N. L. 1961. Statistical comparisons between committed and attempted suicides. In N. L. Farberow and E. S. Shneidman, eds. *The cry for help.* New York: McGraw-Hill Book Company, pp. 129–35.

SMART, R. G., and BATEMAN, K. 1967. Unfavorable reactions to LSD. *Canad. Med. Ass. J.* 97: 1214–21.

STENBACK, A., and BLUMENTHAL, M. 1964. Relationship of alcoholism, hypochondria, and attempted suicide. *Acta. Psychiat. Scand.* 40: 133–40.

STROMGREN, E. 1946. Mental sequelae of suicidal attempts by hanging. *Acta Psychiat. Kbh.* 21: 753–80.

ZMUC, M. 1968. Alcohol and suicide. *Alcoholism* 4: 38–44.

CHAPTER 17

SUICIDE AND MENTAL ILLNESS

In any scientific investigation, one of the first things that must be done is to decide what questions are capable of being answered. There is no point in wasting time on questions which are unanswerable. Making the decision that a question is unanswerable may depend on several factors. First, the question may be stated in a meaningless way (for example, "What makes people tick?"). If it cannot be restated meaningfully, it cannot be answered. Second, there may be no methods available for making the tests which would answer the question. Third, investigating the phenomenon might change the process that would otherwise go on.

One of the most frequently asked questions about suicide—"Are suicidal people insane?"—risks being called unanswerable on all three of the criteria mentioned above. The question as it stands is not meaningful because the word "insane" has no precise meaning for behavioral scientists. (Lawyers might be willing to try to define it, but psychologists, psychiatrists, and sociologists are not.) Some psychologists would define mental illness as a state of abnormal biochemical functioning in the brain. Others would call it a disorder of behavior produced by wrong treatment during childhood. Still others would say that mental illness is simply a way of acting that the person has learned because he was rewarded for it. No matter which of these definitions might be chosen, it would be difficult to tell whether the description were true of a given individual.

Asking whether suicidal people are insane leads to still other problems. One must decide whether the question means, "are they insane in general?" or, "are they insane for a brief period before the suicidal act?" The first meaning of the question suffers from the problems discussed above. The second possibility requires information that is almost impossible to obtain. Other people are rarely aware of a suicide's state of mind and behavior immediately before his act. On occasion, a suicide may talk into a tape recorder while he is dying, or may call a suicide prevention center shortly before death occurs. However, this does not occur in enough cases for any judgments to be made about the sanity of people in the process of committing suicide.

Because the original question about mental illness and suicide cannot be answered, suicidologists have turned to other questions that are relevant in this context.

SUICIDE RATES AMONG THE MENTALLY ILL

One approach to solving this problem is to interview friends and relatives of a person who has completed suicide and to use their evidence in judging whether the suicide's previous behavior was unusual. Estimates of mental illness among suicides gathered by this method range from five to ninety-four percent—a range so large as to be almost meaningless. All of the higher estimates involved interviews with people who knew that the suicide had occurred, a fact which could have biased their judgment. Many people believe that suicide is an insane act; if the interviewees had felt that way, they would have been more likely to say that the suicide was mentally ill. Having committed one "insane" act, he might be seen as generally insane. On the other hand, when objective data collected prior to the suicide are analyzed, the estimates of mental illness are much lower, ranging from about five to twenty-two percent. This evidence suggests that mental illness may be more common in suicidal than in non-suicidal people.

Although no good definition exists for insanity, there are some characteristics related to mental illness which are easy to measure. One important question has to do with whether a person has ever been in a mental hospital. Hospitalization generally indicates that the person has been behaving in some noticeably deviant fashion. Once the person has been hospitalized, records about the diagnosis of his behavior problem are kept. The fact of hospitalization and the patient's diagnosis are two important data to use.

The suicide rate does seem to be higher among those who have been hospitalized than among the rest of the population: 37.0 per 100,000 per year for those who had been hospitalized; 9.6 per 100,000 per year for those who had not (Temoche et al., 1964).

The question of the suicide rate for hospitalized people with different diagnoses is complicated by the meaning of the diagnosis. Each diagnostic category, like schizophrenia or depressive psychosis, is a term that covers a set of behaviors which tend to be found together. It is, most probably, not a term that singles out a particular disease entity. Two cases of schizophrenia do not resemble each other in the way that two cases of measles or chickenpox do. Each schizophrenic's behavior is his own, and it has only general resemblances to that of another schizophrenic. Nonetheless, it is customary to classify people according to diagnosis, both as an aid to psychotherapy and for research purposes.

Although the suicide rates reported for different diagnoses vary from study to study, there is rough agreement on the relative risks. Manic-depressive psychoses have the highest reported rates of completed suicide, while the neuroses have the lowest. (Table 17.1 gives an overview of the suicide rates associated with different diagnoses, as found by one investigation.)

Table 17.1
SUICIDE RATES PER 100,000 PER YEAR
FOR DIFFERENT DIAGNOSTIC CATEGORIES
(POKORNY, 1964)

Alcohol disorders	78
Organic disorders	133
Schizophrenia	167
Depressive psychoses	566
Neuroses—psychosomatic disorders	119
Personality disorders	130

The high rate of completed suicides among manic-depressives is logical. The seriously depressed person sees the world as a totally uninviting place. His view of the possibilities for his life becomes very restricted, since there are few things that seem worth doing. (As we have noted in other chapters, this restriction of alternatives is typical of suicidal thinking.) Eventually, the *ennui* of remaining in a life where nothing is appealing may make the prospect of death and nothingness seem desirable. However, as we pointed out in the first chapter, suicide rarely occurs in the depths of depression. It is much more likely to come about as the depression begins to lift. Perhaps it is only as the person emerges from deepest depression that he has enough energy even to choose death over life.

SPECIFIC SYMPTOMS AND SUICIDE

Although manic-depressives complete suicide more frequently than people with other diagnoses, the table presented above makes it clear that non-depressive patients also kill themselves. An important question to ask is whether, within a diagnostic category, certain behavior symptoms tend to accompany suicidal behavior. Is one kind of schizophrenic behavior almost always accompanied by suicidal behavior, while others never are? Or, do all types of schizophrenic patients have the same suicide rate?

Suicidologists have tried to answer this question for a number of diagnostic categories. Most of the research has failed to find specific symptoms which could be used to predict suicidal behavior. No special symptoms seem to be associated with suicide in schizophrenics. There seem to be no differences in the suicide rates of patients who simply become depressed and of those who alternate depression and euphoria.

One difference was among patients with depressive psychoses (Gittleson, 1966). Some depressive patients have obsessions—uncontrollable thoughts about some topic that recur repeatedly—while others do not. The attempted suicide rate, according to Gittleson, was lowest in the patients who had obsessions and highest in those who did not. 5.9 percent of the obsessive depressed patients attempted suicide, as opposed to 38.2 percent of the non-obsessive depressed patients. In some way, the obsessions may have served as a defense mechanism which protected the patients against suicide. The constant preoccupation with an obsessive idea may keep the patient too busy to think about suicide. The intrusion into his thoughts may prevent him from thinking about anything long enough to take action.

SUICIDAL BEHAVIOR IN NEUROTICS
AND PSYCHOTICS

The neurotic person does not show the extreme deviance of behavior and thought that is found in the psychotic. However, his problems are sufficiently severe to keep him from fully enjoying life or performing at his maximum level. The differences between these two levels of emotional disturbance have led people to ask whether there are differences in the suicidal behavior of neurotics and psychotics.

It has been suggested that psychotics are more prone to complete suicide, while neurotics are more prone to attempt suicide. One writer has said of the neurotic:

> He may play with the idea of suicide intellectually for it is obviously an easy way out but he never uses any force or determination. The windows from which he throws himself are ground floor ones and the ponds in which he would drown himself are those pertaining to ducks (Gordon, 1929, p. 63).

Karl Menninger also subscribed to this view. When talking of neurotic invalids and neurotics he said:

> The fact is, however, that chronic invalids of this type seldom die young, and despite frequent threats of suicide, rarely resort to it (Menninger, 1938, pp. 157–58).

> The neurotic patient rarely mutilates himself irrevocably. Substitute and symbolic forms of self-mutilation are, however, very common. . . . In the neuroses self-castration is usually achieved indirectly, for example, by impotence, financial failure, marital disaster, venereal disease (Menninger, 1938, pp. 234, 308).

Although the relationship between degree of mental illness and type of suicidal behavior has often been suggested, the idea has never been tested empirically. With the data that are presently available, no test is possible, since no study has examined both completed and attempted suicide rates for patients with different diagnoses. If we are willing to approach the problem indirectly, however, there is some relevant evidence available.

Several researchers have investigated the relationship between the lethality of a suicidal act and the diagnosis of the person's problem. Attempted suicides, of course, can vary in lethality; some may not be at all dangerous, while others may barely fail to produce death. The same is true of completed suicides. Some may have been just sufficient to kill, while others involved enough poison or severe enough wounds to kill several people. In most cases, a completed suicide involves more lethal factors than a suicide attempt. It appears that those whose suicidal acts are more lethal are more often psychotic, while those making less lethal attempts are more often neurotic (Dorpat and Boswell, 1963). These findings support the contentions of Gordon and Menninger. But, as we did earlier, we must ask whether the patient's diagnosis was affected by the degree of lethality of his suicidal act.

SEX, SUICIDE, AND MENTAL DISORDER

There is another indirect approach which we can take to the relationship between degree of mental illness and seriousness of suicidal behavior. As mentioned in an earlier chapter, there are sex differences in lethality of suicidal acts. Women tend to attempt suicide, while men tend to complete suicide. If a sex difference in seriousness of mental illness were to exist, this would provide further evidence about the relationship between mental illness and suicide. In fact, there is such a sex difference in rates of mental illness, and it is in the right direction. More men than women are psychotic, and more women than men are neurotic. Table 17.2 gives an example of the number of people in each category in one town.

Table 17.2

THE PREVALENCE OF MENTAL DISORDER IN A
SMALL TOWN. AFTER ROTH AND LUTON (1943).

	Males	*Females*
Psychotic	89	67
Neurotic	39	60

SUICIDES WITH DIFFERENT DIAGNOSES

It appears that people with different emotional disorders are led toward suicide by different motivations. There is no single stress or need which is at work in the suicides of all psychotics. An event that precipitates suicide in one mentally ill person may have little or no effect on another.

A study by Robins and O'Neal (1958) gives a good example of the differences that can exist in the suicidal behavior of different diagnostic groups. The researchers studied two groups of attempted suicides in a large general hospital. Group A had sociopathic personalities, chronic alcoholism, and conversion reactions (physical disabilities which occurred in response to emotional stress). Group B had manic-depressive psychoses and/or chronic brain syndrome. People in Group A had suffered more broken homes as children, and as adults had more divorces, more arrests, more hospitalizations, and more general social disturbances. All of the patients in Group A had had at least one such stress in the six months prior to the suicide attempt, while less than half of the people in Group B had a recent experience of that kind. The people in Group

A were more concerned with their feelings about others at the time of their suicide attempt, while those in Group B were more concerned with their feelings about themselves.

Motivation toward suicide has been examined for a number of specific diagnostic categories. For example, Allen (1967) has discussed the role of the suicidal impulse in paranoia. Allen felt that paranoia (whose principal manifestation is fear of others) is based upon a suicidal desire which accompanies a basic depression. The paranoid patient handles his frightening suicidal wish by attributing the desire to kill him to other people rather than to himself. He then feels somewhat safer, since he can hide from other people. If he perceived the threat as coming from himself, he could never escape from the object of his fear.

A description of psychiatric disturbances that accompany particular suicidal behaviors has been given by Beall (1969).

> In summary, it appears that there are three prominent syndromes— two of suicide attempts and one of suicide. One of the two suicide attempt syndromes is characterized by psychopathic acting-out where impulsivity is prominent, aggressiveness is the typical behavioral mode, there is little evidence of guilt, the method is passive, and where the attempt (which is usually not very harmful) comes without advance warning. This variety occurs more often among the jobless. While this type of impulse-ridden sociopathic attempt is more likely to occur in men, another kind of sham attempt occurs in women with a hysterical personality style. In the latter cases, passivity is the characteristic behavioral mode, there is exaggerated evidence of guilt used in a manipulative way, the method is dramatic, and the attempt usually comes with clear warning to provide for rescue.
>
> In the completed suicide, which occurs more often among professional and managerial people (as compared to the jobless in the sociopathic attempt group) the conflict is more internal, the usual behavioral mode is restricted rather than impulsive and aggressive, and the personality mode is often an obsessive-compulsive one that masks guilt over dependency. Warning is likely but not dramatic, and the method chosen usually more painful. In the restricted, obsessive, depressive personality, the final act is still an impulsive one but there is little in the way of acting; the attempt is serious and the result usually fatal. In the serious obsessive suicide there seems to be a rupture of the superego whereas in the psychopathic attempt, there seems to be little superego restriction to begin with. (Beall, 1969, p. 9)

SUICIDE, SUGGESTIBILITY, AND CONTAGION

If a person is emotionally disturbed, can hearing about a suicide induce him to kill himself? The idea of the suicide "epidemic" is a popular one that stresses the role of imitation in suicidal behavior. Suicides do sometimes appear in clusters, and the acts as a group may resemble one another in method.

When the possibility of imitation is analyzed for groups of suicidal acts, it appears that "contagion" may be at work for the less serious attempts but not for the more lethal acts. One investigator studied an epidemic of suicidal behavior on a Marine base overseas (Hankoff, 1961). The attempts were clustered in time and similar in method. The first attempt in a cluster got maximum benefit in terms of hospitalization and removal from duty. The later attempts gained less, and eventually the behavior ended.

Motto (1967) tried to test the idea that reading newspaper accounts of suicides can precipitate serious suicidal acts. He studied the completed suicide rates in seven cities during newspaper strikes and compared them to the rates over the previous five years. The suicide rate was somewhat lower during the strikes (although not significantly so) in five cities (Baltimore, New York, Cleveland, Portland, and Seattle), but higher in two cities (Detroit and Honolulu). Motto concluded that communication via newspapers had no real influence on suicidal behavior. More recently, Motto noted that the completed suicide rate for women dropped significantly during a nine-month news blackout in Detroit.

CONCLUSION

It is not possible to answer the simple question, "Are suicidal people insane?" However, we can answer other questions that have direct or indirect bearing on the point. The suicide rate is higher among those who have been hospitalized for mental illness. It is highest among patients diagnosed as having a manic-depressive psychosis. For some diagnostic categories, it is possible to find some symptoms which tend to accompany suicidal behavior, but this is not the case for all kinds of mental illness. In general, the neurotic patient attempts suicide, while the psychotic completes the act. There is no evidence that suggestibility can trigger serious suicidal behavior in the emotionally disturbed, though imitation may play some role in less lethal acts.

BIBLIOGRAPHY

ALLEN, T. E. 1967. Suicidal impulse in depression and paranoia. *Int. J. Psychoan.* 48: 433–38.

BEALL, L. 1969. The dynamics of suicide. *Bull. Suicidol.* March: 2–16.

DORPAT, T., and BOSWELL, J. W. 1963. An evaluation of suicidal intent in suicide attempts. *Comp. Psychiat.* 4: 117–25.

GITTLESON, N. L. 1966. The relationship between obsessions and suicidal attempts in depressive psychoses. *Brit. J. Psychiat.* 112: 889–90.

GORDON, R. G. 1929. Certain personality problems in relation to mental illness with special reference to suicide and homicide. *Brit. J. Med. Psychol.* 9: 60–66.

HANKOFF, L. D. 1961. An epidemic of attempted suicide. *Comp. Psychiat.* 2: 294–98.

MENNINGER, K. 1938. *Man against himself.* New York: Harcourt Brace Jovanovich, Inc.

MOTTO, J. A. 1967. Suicide and suggestibility. *Amer. J. Psychiat.* 124: 252–56.

POKORNY, A. D. 1964. Suicide rates in various psychiatric disorders. *J. Nerv. Ment. Dis.* 139: 499–506.

ROBINS, E., and O'NEAL, P. 1958. Culture and mental disorder. *Human Organization* 16 (4): 7–11.

ROTH, W. F., and LUTON, F. H. 1943. The mental health program in Tennessee. *Amer. J. Psychiat.* 99: 662–75.

TEMOCHE, A., PUGH, T. F., and MACMAHON, B. Suicide rates among current and former mental institution patients. *J. Nerv. Ment. Dis.* 138: 124–30.

CHAPTER 18

TIME, SEASON, WEATHER, AND SUICIDE

Naïve theories of suicide often assert that suicide is more likely at certain times or when certain weather conditions exist. Various times, some of them mutually exclusive, are thought of as unusually likely occasions for suicide: Christmas or other holidays, winter, spring, anniversaries of loved ones' deaths. Night is thought of as a more likely time than day. Weather conditions, too, are seen as setting an appropriate stage for suicide; bad weather is seen as depressing, while the high suicide rate in California has led people to implicate good weather as well. Dr. Arnold Stoper once suggested, in conversation, his own theory—that during bad weather people blame their depression on the weather, and when good weather comes they lose their excuse. This inability to externalize blame increases the chance that they will kill themselves. He explained the high California suicide rate by saying that there is rarely bad weather, so people are rarely able to blame their depression on external sources such as the weather.

In recent years, suicidologists have tried to test the many possibilities for relationships between the occurrence of suicides and temporal or meteorological variables. Let us examine some of the work that has been done.

144

SEASONAL RHYTHMS AND SUICIDE

It has long been recognized that there is a seasonal variation in the rate of completed suicide. Louis Dublin has noted that between 1910 and 1923 the variation was quite clear. The peak number of suicides occurred in May, with the rate then falling month by month to its low in December. (The difference was statistically significant.) The seasonal variation was more marked in rural than in urban areas. More recently, according to Dublin's investigations, the pattern has changed. The peak is still in April or May and the low point in December, but the variation is less clear than it was, and there are subsidiary peaks. Perhaps this change is related to increasing urbanization of the population.

If the suicide rate really does follow some seasonal trend, there should be a reverse pattern in the Southern Hemisphere from that in the Northern. Dublin investigated seasonal variations in Australia for three separate years, but found little consistency of peaks and troughs. Other workers have reported a peak during the Australian spring (September and October), but their results were not statistically significant.

It remains somewhat unclear just what the relation is between the seasons and the suicide rate. Perhaps there is a seasonal variation for deaths of all kinds, and suicide does not stand in any special relationship to the seasons (although David Lester's data do not support this theory). The early suicidologist Durkheim suggested that a seasonal variation might be due to differences in social activity during the different seasons. It seems premature to speculate on this theory, however, because we are still unsure about the seasonal suicide pattern.

SUICIDE AND HOLIDAYS

P. H. Blachly and N. Fairly (1969) studied the incidence of suicide on holidays. Most people's implicit theories would predict a high holiday suicide rate because an unhappy person feels left out of the celebration, or, alternatively, a low rate because the potential suicide is busy with holiday activity. Blachly and Fairly found high suicide rates for some holidays (for example, Pearl Harbor Day—a holiday not noted for elaborate festivities) and low rates for others (such as Memorial Day). However, the suicide rate for all holidays combined was not significantly different from that for the whole year.

DAY OF THE WEEK AND SUICIDE

Intuition seems to suggest that some days of the week are more likely to have a high suicide rate than others. "Blue" Monday, when people must return to work or school after the weekend, might be considered an especially dangerous time. Most studies on this topic have yielded highly conflicting data. Blachly and Fairly attempted a more complex analysis than is usually done. Rather than looking simply at all suicides lumped together in relation to day of the week, they divided the suicides they were investigating into two groups: people between forty and sixty-four years of age, and those between birth and thirty-nine or over sixty-five years of age. They found a high incidence of suicide on Mondays for the first group, but no specific trend for the second group.

TIME OF DAY AND SUICIDE

As noted above, night is often thought of as the time when suicide occurs. This assumption is shown by the importance which suicide prevention centers often place on twenty-four-hour availability. However, Edwin Shneidman and Norman Farberow have found that significantly more suicides occur between noon and 6:00 P.M., and significantly fewer between midnight and 6:00 A.M. The findings of other workers have supported this general pattern. (However, it is not always possible to determine exactly when a suicidal act occurred, so these results are based on incomplete samples.)

THE WEATHER AND SUICIDE

Early work on the relationship between weather and suicide rates concentrated largely on finding logical reasons for hypothesized associations rather than empirically investigating the association. An early suggestion was that hot, humid, and windy weather causes extensive low-grade skin irritation and thus makes the nervous system more irritable, increasing the likelihood of suicide. The same author (Phillips, 1909) suggested that the annual variation in the quality and quantity of foods eaten might produce an association between the suicide rate and the weather. A somewhat later hypothesis (Hopkins, 1937) stated more reasonably that social activity varied with the weather and was responsible for any relation between weather and suicide rate. It is hard to say, though, whether there should be more social activity during bad weather (when people stay at home) or during good (when they go out more).

It is only in recent years that empirical investigations of the association between weather and suicide rate have been done. Much of this work has been done by A. D. Pokorny and his associates in Houston, Texas. They have examined the relationships between rates of completed and of attempted suicide and eleven weather variables (temperature, wind speed, wind direction, barometric pressure, relative humidity, visibility, ceiling height, rain, fog, thunderstorms, and cloudiness). When the data were controlled for differences in frequency of weather conditions in the course of a year, no significant relationships were found between any of the variables and the rates of either attempted or completed suicide. Passage of a cold front was not associated with any change in incidence of suicide, either on the day of passage or on the days before and after passage.

E. Digon and H. B. Bock, working in Philadelphia (1966), found much the same lack of evidence for association between weather conditions and suicide. They reported two positive associations, however. A high relative humidity with an atmospheric pressure of thirty millimeters of mercury was associated with a low suicide rate. A high rate occurred on days when there was a marked change in barometric pressure. Pokorny repeated this test and found no significant association. He pointed out that Digon and Bock's results could have occurred because of statistical complications rather than because of a genuine correlation.

THE MOON, THE SUN, AND SUICIDE

A relationship between the moon and behavioral disturbances has long been suspected by folk wisdom. Severe emotional disturbances have been attributed to the influence of the moon to such an extent that the word "lunacy" is derived from the Latin word for "moon." Werewolves were thought to change from man to wolf under the influence of the full moon. A person who is vague and unalert may be called "moonstruck." With all these folk beliefs about the power of the moon, it was inevitable that suicidologists would investigate the relationship between moon phase and suicide rate.

Pokorny (1964) studied all completed suicides in Texas during 1959–61, and noted for each the phase of the moon and the point on the apogee-perigee cycle. No significant relationships were found for the whole sample of suicides or for subgroups of sex or race. Nor was there a correlation between suicidal behavior and the day preceding perigee. David Lester investigated the association for completed suicides in Erie

County, New York, during 1964–68 and again found no reliable correlation.

Pokorny (1966b) also investigated the relationship between sunspot activity and rate of suicide, but found no correlation even when he allowed for a possible lag of several days between sunspots and the suicidal act.

CONCLUSION

It must be concluded that all this painstaking work has yielded little positive knowledge about suicide. Some seasonal variation seems possible, and a relationship to time of day seems fairly clear; however, weather, holidays, the phase of the moon, and the occurrence of sunspots do not seem related to the suicide rate.

BIBLIOGRAPHY

BLACHLY, P. H., and FAIRLEY, N. 1969. Market analysis for suicide prevention. *Northwest Med.* 68: 232–38.

DIGON, E., and BOCK, H. B. 1966. Suicide and climatology. *Arch. Environ. Hlth.* 12: 278–86.

DUBLIN, L. 1963. *Suicide.* New York: The Ronald Press Company.

DURKHEIM, E. 1951. *Suicide.* Glencoe, Ill.: The Free Press.

EDWARDS, J. E., and WHITLOCK, F. A. 1968. Suicide and attempted suicide in Brisbane. *Med. J. Austral.* 1: 932–38.

HOPKINS, F. 1937. Attempted suicide. *J. Ment. Sci.* 83: 71–94.

LESTER, D., BROCKOPP, G. N., and PRIEBE, K. 1969. Association between a full moon and attempted suicide. *Psychol. Rep.* 25: 598.

PHILLIPS, W. R. F. 1909. Seasonal influences on suicide. *Trans. Amer. Clin. Climatol. Ass.* 25: 156–66.

POKORNY, A. D. 1964. Moon phases, suicide, and homicide. *Amer. J. Psychiat.* 212: 66–67.

——— 1966a. Suicide and weather. *Arch. Environ. Hlth.* 13: 255–56.

——— 1966b. Sunspots, suicides and homicide. *Dis. Nerv. Syst.* 27: 347–48.

POKORNY, A. D., DAVIS, F., and HARBERSON, W. 1963. Suicide, suicide attempts and weather. *Amer. J. Psychiat.* 120: 377–81.

SHNEIDMAN, E. S., and FARBEROW, N. L. 1961. Statistical comparsions between committed and attempted suicides. In N. L. Farberow and E. S. Shneidman, eds. *The cry for help.* New York: McGraw-Hill Book Company, pp. 19–47.

CHAPTER 19

A CASE OF SUICIDE

A single case of suicide does not provide enough information to allow us to draw conclusions about suicides in general. On the other hand, for the reader who is not experienced with suicidal behavior, the statistics derived through research may seem dry and unrelated to real people. For this reason we think it may be beneficial to present a psychological autopsy. A psychological autopsy is not simply a case record. It is a research method that tries to determine the psychological processes which terminated in a person's death. Much information that is not relevant to the dynamics of the suicide may be available about an individual; the psychological autopsy, unlike a case record, is directed primarily toward the emotional processes that moved the suicide toward his death. Information about these processes is gathered through interviews with friends and relatives of the completed suicide after his death. In our presentation, we will first report the information given by those who had known the dead man, and then discuss some of the details in terms of research findings reported elsewhere in this book.[1]

[1] We are very grateful to Dr. Gene W. Brockopp, Executive Director of the Suicide Prevention and Crisis Service of Erie County, for allowing us to use this case material. The case did not come from Erie County. Names and other identifying information have been changed where necessary.

THE SUICIDE OF THOMAS McCLEARY

Thomas McCleary killed himself in his apartment at the age of about thirty-one by cutting his throat and bleeding to death. Information about his life and his activities just before his suicide was obtained through interviews with his girl friend, his mother, and a close male friend.

STATEMENT OF
CHRISTINE BLASZKOPANICK

Christine was twenty-eight years old and divorced several times. She had two children in foster homes. She had been hospitalized briefly for an emotional disturbance. Christine was of Polish extraction and attractive, but slightly overweight. Her use of language and vocabulary indicated above-average intelligence. She showed little emotion. She and Tom McCleary had met in a bar and had immediately begun to live together; at the time of the interview she was four months pregnant with his child. Tom and she had planned to be married in December (about two weeks after the suicide).

When Christine was asked to describe Tom's personality, she stressed his insecurity and the tensions which he kept under control with drugs and alcohol. The feeling of insecurity seemed to be based on problems from his early life: the fact that he differed from most people he knew in that he had never been baptized; the lack of presence of a father in his family, due to divorce; and the feeling that he could never trust anyone because he had not been able to trust his father. Tom enjoyed questioning Christine about her past and making negative remarks about it. However, during most of the time that they were alone together, she characterized him as being "warm, gentle, understanding, sensitive, kind, and intelligent." When they were with other people, he behaved quite differently, being cold, distant, and critical of Christine, as well as rude to other people. He intensely disliked the feeling that other people were false or that another person was superior to him.

Christine felt that Tom was constantly struggling with inner conflicts and tensions. He usually managed to keep these under control, but they would become apparent in anxieties, depressions, physical twitches, or violent behavior. At times his hands would become immobile or would twitch, or his face would go into spasms. When this happened, Tom would get something to drink or take some pills. He was constantly drinking beer and smoking. At times, he would also be violent. He said he could kill someone if he had to. When Christine and he disagreed, he would hit her, then look surprised, apologizing and begging her not to leave him. (Often she did leave after a quarrel, but she always returned in a day or two.)

According to Christine, Tom had only a few friends; "he could not stand people and would drive them away." The only long-term friend he had was George Adams, whose statement about Tom appears below. When Christine was asked about Tom's relationship with George, she became very agitated and wanted to be assured that George would never see the statement she was making. When the interviewer reassured her, she stated that Tom had disliked George somewhat, but that George was always there when Tom needed him. George was "attracted to Tom," but they did not have a homosexual relationship. However, Tom had told her that before she came to live with him, George had tried to "fondle" him twice when he was drunk. On a number of occasions, George had taken off all his clothes and lain next to Tom. Once, Christine had hidden in the closet when George came to see Tom and had heard George tell how he liked to go to the gym and see the men's bodies. Christine had asked George to stop seeing Tom for a few months, but George had declared that Tom needed him. George had become very angry when told that Christine and Tom were going to get married. He had actually been supporting both of them, but indicated to Christine at Tom's funeral that he did not care to go on helping her.

As far as Christine knew, Tom had made no previous suicide threats or attempts while they were living together. She recalled that a few weeks previous to his death, he remarked that if a person wanted to kill someone, it was not hard: "just go from here to here with a razor." He drew his finger from ear to ear across his neck.

Christine gave a description of the events leading to Tom's suicide. He began drinking vodka heavily on a Sunday in November and continued to drink throughout the next week. At the same time, he took Dexamil. He kept drinking and taking the drug until he was unconscious; as soon as he woke up, he began again. He pawned his possessions to get money and talked about robbing a liquor store to get more to drink. He kept saying he would "taper off tomorrow," but never did so. On Tuesday, Christine said, she told him she could not take it any more and left, but she returned on Wednesday and stayed until Friday. On Wednesday, Tom took lighted cigarettes and put them out by pressing them against his body. He told Christine, "I would ask you to do it to me but I know you wouldn't do it." On Friday, Christine told Tom she "could not marry him as he was," and left again. He did not respond emotionally to her statement, but walked her downstairs, "acting kind of goofy," according to Christine, and talking about a gun. She returned on Friday night and found that the door was chained. This and some other circumstances disturbed Christine, since Tom had told her before that he only chained the door when he felt someone was after him or when he was afraid he would hurt someone. Tom went out for a bottle and Christine left, though she had told him she would wait for him. On Saturday, he was looking for her and told George Adams he thought she had left for good. On Sunday, Christine called the Adamses and was told that Tom had killed himself.

STATEMENT OF GEORGE ADAMS

George Adams was a self-employed architect, a self-assured and quiet-spoken man. He appeared to be a devoted husband and father, and was active in church work.

George met Tom McCleary about five years before the latter's death, in a chance encounter on the street as he was going to a local men's club. A few days later he ran into Tom again. Since it was raining, George offered to share his umbrella; this was the beginning of their friendship.

According to George, this chance friendship was motivated by the attractiveness of Tom's personality. Tom "was commanding, he dressed well, he was an outstanding individual, he had a spectacular personality, physical beauty, and a way of handling himself." George felt that he was Tom's only friend, that Tom didn't have friends because "he took advantage of anyone he came in contact with." Although George realized that he, too, was perhaps being taken advantage of, he did not resent it. Instead, he said he regarded Tom "as my son, as a problem child." (Mrs. Adams interrupted at this statement to say that she "hated his [Tom's] guts.")

In line with George's stated paternal feelings toward Tom, he was concerned with the fact that Tom "never really had a chance" because of his family's confused home life, which left the boy on his own from the age of twelve or thirteen. George hoped to give Tom a better sense of values, since he had such "great potential, such a magnetic personality, and was so very charming." According to George, Tom "rejected all things of constructive nature . . . ; [he] indulged himself in whatever he wanted to do; . . . he lived only for the moment." Tom was always "full of wild threats" and "spoke of being dead before he was thirty," but, George said, "I pooh-poohed the idea." In spite of these quirks, "Tom made an outstanding appearance in any group" and inspired such regard in George that he became Tom's "sole source of income, . . . paid the landlord, bought him food, took him out to eat, but rarely gave him money."

George had become involved in Tom's relationships with his family and knew a good deal about them. He had twice paid for Tom's mother to come from Arkansas on visits, during which she stayed with the Adams family. On at least one occasion, he took Tom to Arkansas to visit his mother. George felt that Tom loved his mother, who was a "competent and intelligent woman" employed as a draftsman. Tom's father, on the other hand, was the object of Tom's hatred, since he had abused and rejected Tom during his boyhood. Tom spoke little of his older sister, but was proud of his younger brother, who was studying for an advanced degree.

George also involved himself in Tom's relationships with women. He hired a lawyer on Tom's behalf in order to start divorce proceedings against Tom's wife, but did not think that Tom ever went through with this.

During the five years George knew Tom, the latter was involved in a number of escapades. In most of the cases, George offered support, paid fines, and made himself generally useful. Tom was jailed for drunkenness, and for armed assault and robbery. He was hospitalized several times and attempted suicide on one of these occasions.

George was in close contact with Tom during the week prior to his death. Tom appeared depressed during this time, which George attributed to Christine's having left and to the pressures George was putting on him to go into the hospital. George also felt that the Thanksgiving holiday was difficult for Tom since he was "alone without food or money and . . . drinking heavily." George managed to get Tom to make a brief visit to an alcoholism clinic on the day before Thanksgiving, when Tom was "in bad shape; . . . incoherent."

On the following Saturday night, Tom called George to ask to be taken to the hospital. George returned the call a little later to make sure Tom was still willing to go, at which time Tom said he would not go. Three calls in four hours came from Tom. At the time of the last call, Tom told George, "I want to see you and be with you." Since Tom still refused to go to the hospital, however, George did not visit him. At 8:30 the next morning George went to Tom's apartment to check on him. Tom said that he felt awful and was ready to go to the hospital; he was lying in bed, fully dressed but unshaven and puffy-faced.

The two went by car to a well-known private hospital, but when they got there, Tom said, "I'm not going in. I'm afraid. They won't take me here." George agreed that they probably would not admit Tom, and asked where he wanted to go. Tom named a nearby state hospital and said he would go in if taken there. Once they arrived at the hospital, Tom again refused to go in, saying that he was afraid. George acquiesced, telling Tom, "I can understand that, it would have been painful . . . I won't force you."

By this time it was late and George wanted to go to church, so he took

Tom back to his apartment. Tom asked him not to leave, then to buy him a drink. The drink was refused, but George agreed to stay for a few minutes. When George finally left, Tom asked whether he would come back, and he said he would be back around 3 o'clock.

At 3 P.M., George came back with some sandwiches for Tom and had to use his key to get in. He noticed blood on the bed and then found the body in the bathroom.

STATEMENT OF
MILLICENT McCLEARY

Tom's mother looked younger than her age and was conservatively dressed. She was quiet and controlled and talked about Tom in a detached voice. Only toward the end of the interview did she show any emotion.

Mrs. McCleary was divorced and remarried to the same man three times. The divorces occurred when Tom was seven, eleven and a half, and fourteen years old. Tom's father, Steven McCleary, was a writer. The mother described him as an alcoholic and a man who "didn't want a family." There were two children other than Tom: a slightly older sister and a brother five and a half years younger.

Mrs. McCleary remembered her son as a large, healthy baby whose early development was normal. However, he became a solemn child who played by himself. Only at the age of ten or eleven did he begin to "go to the end of the block and play with other boys." He was a poor loser at games. Mrs. McCleary was told that Tom had a high I.Q. However, he was expelled from every school he went to. In the tenth grade, he was barely passing.

Tom's relationship with his father during this period was very poor. The father "was always picking at him and asking embarrassing questions." The mother felt that a "father is always jealous of his older son." She vividly recalled an incident between Tom and his father when the former was thirteen years old. "His father was drunk and Tom pinned him against the corner of the wall and beat his face until it was unrecognizable . . . this is where Tom tore everything down . . . he could never look up to his father again."

When Tom was fourteen, he was sent to a reformatory for thirteen months. According to his mother, there were no specific charges filed against him, but he would "roam in the streets until 2 A.M.," he "hid guns," and he was "accused of street fighting."

When Tom was fifteen, his mother took him to a psychiatrist for treatment. He left school during this year. He also shot himself in the stomach with a rifle and had to have his spleen removed. He later let his mother know it was a deliberate act. After he recovered, he had several jobs with local businesses.

Tom joined the Army at the age of seventeen with his mother's permission. He received an honorable discharge after two years. Mrs. McCleary felt that he liked the Army and did well during this time. Upon leaving the army, he went to live with his former psychiatrist for a year, and then got his own apartment. (Although Mrs. McCleary approved of Tom's Army experience, she seemed resentful and anxious about his relationship with the psychiatrist.)

Tom got married at twenty-three or twenty-four and had two children. Mrs. McCleary thought that the couple were divorced two years before Tom's death. She never saw her daughter-in-law or grandchildren, although she frequently talked to Tom on the telephone at this time.

Mrs. McCleary last saw Tom two years before his death, when he visited her at home. She felt at the time that he had changed. He did not want to be seen with his brother for fear that he might embarrass the brother and his friends. He twice crushed a glass in his bare hands. He was drinking heavily.

Looking back over Tom's adulthood, Mrs. McCleary felt that he "didn't get along with anyone very well; he had no friends over a year or two except Mr. Adams." She thought that that friendship was maintained only because of George Adams' patience and the trouble he took. She said of Tom that "he had everything—looks, brains, talent . . . ," that "he was afraid to let anyone close to him . . . ," that "he was a complex person" who "someways . . . almost quit growing somewhere back there." Mrs. McCleary frequently referred to her son as "poor little Tom —he will always be my little boy."

The last time Mrs. McCleary talked to Tom was about two weeks before his death. He called to introduce her to Christine, to tell her about his plans for getting married, and to ask for $300 to come to Arkansas. Although she had given him money before, she refused this time. She felt he had been drinking heavily at the time of the telephone call.

In talking about Tom's suicide, his mother said he must have felt, because "he was afraid to let anyone get close to him," that "there was no use staying around . . . that it's going to end some day so let's end it now." She became angry and said that she could understand homicide but could not understand someone who wanted to die. She was not planning to tell Tom's brother and sister that he had committed suicide. She would just say he got his "pills and alcohol mixed; no one will know for sure." It seemed to the interviewer that she was trying to protect herself and Tom from reality.

COMMENTS ON THE CASE
OF THOMAS McCLEARY

Like every individual case of completed suicide, that of Tom McCleary has unique qualities. Tom was a person like no other person and cannot be compared to other suicides on all possible characteristics. Nevertheless, when we examine the case, we can note that Tom shared a number of characteristics with completed suicides as a group.

FAMILY BACKGROUND
AND RELATIONSHIPS

Like many other completed suicides, Tom McCleary came from a highly unstable family. The parents' three divorces and remarriages are evidence of the constantly changing home life encountered by their son. When the parents were together, the father's alcoholism and aloofness from the family destroyed any chances for a good relationship between him and Tom. The two relatively good relationships between Tom and members of his family were also distant ones. He was fond of his younger brother, but in the later years of his life refused to be seen with him for fear of embarrassing him—an indication that the relationship was not a truly intimate one. He maintained contact with his mother and said that he loved her, but she never met his wife or children.

SOCIAL RELATIONSHIPS

All of the informants confirmed that Tom had few friends and that the friendships he developed were usually brief. His relationship with Christine does not appear to have been a deeply intimate one, beginning as it did with a casual pick-up and being maintained apparently as a drinking companionship. The friendship with George was maintained primarily through George's own efforts. George's motivation for keeping up the relationship is not clear; if Christine's statements are true, homosexual elements as well as altruistic ones were involved. In any case, the friendship was not a matter of mutual affection and support, as far as we can tell.

PREVIOUS SUICIDAL ACTS

As noted elsewhere, the past of a completed suicide often shows previous suicidal acts, suicide threats, and other forms of self-destructive behavior. The statements of Tom McCleary's friends and relatives show that Tom behaved in these ways from an early age. His mother reported his shooting himself in the stomach at the age of fifteen. George Adams informed the interviewer that Tom had attempted suicide during one of his periods of hospitalization. Several weeks before he completed suicide, Tom had described to Christine how easy it would be to kill a person by cutting his throat (the very method he used himself).

Tom's self-destructive behavior is manifest in other behaviors: a consistent pattern of expulsion from schools, teenage delinquency, drunkenness, armed robbery, and drug use as an adult.

EMOTIONAL DISTURBANCE

Tom first received psychiatric treatment in his teens. As an adult, he was hospitalized several times and became sufficiently familiar with the local mental health system to know which hospitals would accept him and which would not.

LOSS OF SOCIAL RELATIONSHIPS

Tom's early life involved repeated losses of his father through divorce. Even when the father was present, his aloofness and heavy drinking made the family virtually fatherless. Later, divorce separated Tom from his wife and children, leaving him relatively isolated, since his friendships and relationships with his family were not intense. The pattern of loss culminated at a crucial time with the departure of Christine, an event which probably played an important role in the triggering of suicide at that particular time. Although Christine claimed that Tom should have known she would return, George's statement indicated that Tom was convinced she had gone for good.

GEORGE'S COMPLICITY

In the following chapter we note that people close to a suicidal individual may actually cooperate with him to bring about his death. George Adams seems to have played such a role in Tom's suicide. Perhaps the clearest evidence for this lies in George's description of his visits with Tom to hospitals just before the suicide. It must have been obvious that Tom was in a highly disturbed state, and that he wished to be hospitalized at the same time that he feared it. George, who was aware of Tom's previous hospitalizations and of one suicide attempt, did not encourage Tom to go to the hospital. He agreed to take him if asked, but, in fact, cast doubt on Tom's decision to go by telephoning to ask whether he was still sure he wanted to go. When Tom finally asked to be driven to a hospital, George, according to his own account, did not urge him to go in. On the contrary, he agreed with Tom's negative statements about the hospitals—that the first probably would not admit him and that it would be very painful to go into the second. (This behavior, in addition to his earlier refusal to visit Tom unless the latter agreed to go to the hospital, seems to indicate a double-binding tendency that may have been characteristic of the relationship.) When the two returned to Tom's apartment, George refused to miss church in order to comply with Tom's urgent request that he stay, although he had previously made many sacrifices of time and money for Tom's sake.

Considering that George's behavior may have been an encouragement for Tom's suicide, we may ask what possible advantage Tom's death could have had for George. Christine's statement about George's homosexual interest, if true, could provide the key here. George's involvement with Tom was a deep one in terms of the responsibility he had taken on. This must have been rewarding in sexual terms, for it brought the two men into close contact. On the other hand, the relationship must have caused George some emotional trouble. His wife disliked Tom intensely and undoubtedly resented money being spent on him and Christine. More important, George must have had some serious conflicts about his homosexual feelings, which one would not expect to be accepted calmly by the average man. At the same time that contact with Tom was sexually pleasurable, it would have aroused stronger and stronger homosexual desires, producing ever greater conflicts. George was probably caught between the rewards and punishments of his situation in such a way that escape seemed difficult. We certainly do not suggest that George planned or consciously wished Tom's death, but the suicide did provide a solution to his problem.

BIBLIOGRAPHY

WEISMAN, A. D., and KASTENBAUM, R. 1968. The psychological autopsy: a study of the terminal phase of life. *Comm. Ment. Hlth. J. Monog.*, 4: 1–59.

CHAPTER 20

RESOURCES FOR PREVENTING SUICIDE

In the effort to prevent suicide, there are a number of possible sources of help for the person whose life is in danger. Of course, a person can at times come to grips with his problems on his own and succeed in emerging unharmed from his suicidal crisis; but this cannot be counted on. For most suicidal people, help from others is very desirable for adequate solution of the problems that are drawing them toward suicide.

THE ROLE OF FAMILY AND FRIENDS

The most convenient and potentially most helpful resources are the friends and relatives of the suicidal person. These people are constantly available, there are no financial restrictions on contact with them, and they have considerable knowledge of the suicidal person's past history. In addition, comfort and counsel from them cannot be seen as "paid friendship," as contact with a professional therapist is sometimes interpreted. If friends and relatives are sensitive and aware of some elementary facts about suicide (like those described in Chapter 1), they may be able to do a great deal for the suicidal person. There are a number of ideas that should be kept in mind when dealing with the potential suicide.

1. The person's feelings must not be denied, but must be accepted as an important part of the situation. If the person says he feels worthless, it is not useful, and it may be destructive, to reassure him that he is ob-

jectively not worthless. He is not being distressed by objective facts or data, but rather by his feelings. Though worthlessness may not be an objective fact, it is a subjective reality and thus a true part of the problem. Similarly, if the person says he wants to die, it is not useful to respond, "Oh, you don't *really* want to die—you're exaggerating." It may be true that death is not his real goal, but he is using a convention of language to try to communicate a true feeling. If another person informs him that what he says is not true, the potential suicide may be confirmed in his notion that no one understands or cares for him. Thus, denial of a feeling may actually be harmful. It is certainly not therapeutic, because the suicidal person is trying to talk in the language of subjective rather than objective reality.

2. The suicidal person is confused about what he wants and how to get it. One of his greatest needs is for others to help him clarify his own internal state. Often, this can be done through talking about feelings, whether the feelings are expressed verbally or communicated by gesture or facial expression. The suicidal person may come to understand his own feelings better simply by talking to someone and listening to his own words ("How do I know what I think till I see what I say?"). A friend or family member may also further the process of clarification by the technique called *reflection of feelings*. In discussion with the suicidal person, the friend should restate the feelings inherent in the comments made by the potential suicide. He should not simply parrot the phrase or the objective facts that are mentioned, but instead should try to understand the implied feelings and respond with a restatement of those. For example, the suicidal person might say, "I can't ever seem to get a date, and when I do the girl is a real dog. There just aren't any nice girls around." A friend might respond to this by saying, "You'd like a girlfriend and you feel lonely without one, but you're afraid you'll never be able to get together with a girl and have a real relationship." This response is in terms of the suicidal person's feelings, not in terms of the objective fact that the supply of nice girls really has not decreased.

3. Since suicide is a "taboo topic," the suicidal person may avoid talking directly about his suicidal plans and wishes. He may want to avoid alienating the person he is talking to, and he needs to be assured that his friend does not consider suicidal tendencies disgusting or morally reprehensible. The friend can make this reassurance by avoiding euphemism and talking directly about suicide. To ask, "Are you thinking of killing yourself?" is far more useful than to say, "You aren't thinking about doing something to yourself, are you?" The latter question invites the potential suicide to lie and to conclude that the friend is not a real source of help. Similar direct questions, such as inquiries into the prospective method of suicide and how long suicide has been contemplated, will help bring out the potential suicide's feelings and will also allow the friend to judge the seriousness of suicidal intent. The friend

should not let social delicacy deter him from discussing specific details about suicidal behavior. It is a myth that talking about suicide to a distressed individual can lead him to kill himself.

PROFESSIONAL HELP

Although friends and family can be very useful in helping the suicidal person, it must also be recognized that there are times when their intervention will not help. Sometimes, of course, friends and relatives are intimately involved in the disturbance that is leading toward suicide. As indicated in Chapter 9, disturbed social relations are frequent among suicidal people. In such cases, a person outside the tangle of unhappy relationships may be the only one who can work productively with the suicidal person. Again, friends and relatives may be too anxious, or temperamentally unsuited to dealing with the difficult problems of a potential suicide; they may become impatient or agitated in spite of the best intentions. They may even have reason to benefit by the person's suicide. Finally, a suicidal person may be seriously disturbed and beyond the skills of a nonprofessional.

In such cases, there are a number of other resources to which the potential suicide and those concerned about him can turn. First, family service organizations, which are found in almost every community, can offer counselors who will ascertain the seriousness of suicidal risk and recommend a course of action. They may suggest family counseling, individual or group therapy with a psychiatrist or clinical psychologist, or, in extreme cases, hospitalization. If an individual therapist is seen, therapy may be brief and crisis-oriented or it may continue over a long period of time.

It should be noted that neither the psychotherapist nor a family counselor may necessarily be free of anxiety over suicide as a "taboo topic." Many therapists and counselors do not feel at home with suicidal patients and prefer to avoid taking them. The anxiety connected with the possibility of a patient's suicide may be overwhelming for the therapist.

SUICIDE PREVENTION CENTERS

In an increasing number of communities, special professionally-run suicide prevention centers have been set up. Such centers may differ widely in nature, but they have in common a special regard for the problems of the suicidal person and special training for dealing with him. Therapists and counselors who work in suicide prevention centers are obviously self-selected for their willingness to work with suicidal patients. Often the centers are partly staffed by volunteer workers, who are trained to accept suicidal behavior as a fact that can be coped with, rather than as a fearful mystery.

Perhaps the best way to communicate how a suicide center works is to describe the functions of a specific center, the Suicide Prevention and Crisis Center, Inc. of Erie County, New York, which is based in Buffalo. The SPCS is a private agency that has a contract with Erie County to run its suicide prevention program. (Previous to the inception of the SPCS in 1968, Buffalo had a non-professional, volunteer suicide prevention organization.) The SPCS has a professional staff consisting of an Executive Director, a Research Director, a Clinical Director, and a Training Director. There are also a number of professional therapists, primarily psychologists and social workers. In addition, there are two very important groups who deal directly with patients: the full-time lay counselors, a group of people with less than a college education who have been given special training at the Center; and the volunteers, people of many kinds, from medical students to housewives and teenagers, who contribute services part-time.

The primary service offered by the SPCS is a twenty-four-hour telephone therapy service. At least one worker is always at the Center to talk to people who call in to discuss their problems. During the hours when demand is heavy, there may be four or five counselors available. The full-time lay counselors take phone calls primarily during the day, while the volunteers remain at the Center all night to answer calls.

Patients call on several lines, which are differentiated in that they are advertised in different ways and probably attract different callers: The Suicide Prevention Line, the Teenage Hot Line, and the Problems in Living Line. In the course of a month, telephone counselors talk to about 2000 patients and answer another 2000 incomplete calls where the caller hangs up immediately or makes obscene or humorous remarks and then hangs up.

The telephone therapists are trained to use many of the same techniques that were recommended earlier in this chapter for the family and friends of the suicidal person. Their principal aim is to help the caller come to grips with his own feelings and reach his own solution for his problems. Reflection of feelings and the asking of questions at appropriate times are methods used to guide the caller's thinking in a constructive direction. The telephone counselors quickly lose their feeling that suicide is a taboo subject and they become able to talk very directly to suicidal callers about their desire for death. As pointed out earlier, many psychotherapists are very ill at ease with suicidal patients and fear that completed suicides will be "their fault." This anxiety is partly due to the fact that the ordinary therapist sees rather few suicidal patients and has little experience with them. The telephone therapist who works with large numbers of suicidal patients soon becomes comfortable with the problem. Furthermore, he soon acquires a vast fund of experience in working with suicidal and distressed individuals and so becomes very capable of helping them.

Naturally, the position of the telephone therapist is a difficult one. The patient can always break off the contact by hanging up, so it is up to the therapist to make sure that his timing and understanding are good. (The patient in face-to-face therapy can also walk out, of course, but that cannot be done instantaneously and without embarrassment and so is much less likely to happen.) The therapist must also manage to get information from and communicate with a person who is in crisis and may be crying uncontrollably or unable to talk coherently. The caller may bring a great deal of suspicion to the encounter and spend much time demanding whether the line is tapped and whether the counselor is qualified to do therapy.

In addition to these difficulties, which are inherent in doing telephone therapy, there is the problem that the counselor may have to handle several calls simultaneously. If calls come in on many lines at once, the therapist must ask some to hold the line while he talks to others. This can become complicated in terms of remembering the problems of people the therapist has talked to only briefly.

If a caller is in a severely suicidal state, says that he has a loaded gun, or has already taken pills or cut himself, the telephone therapist may decide that the situation demands active intervention. The therapists themselves never leave this particular center to go to a patient (although the SPCS is planning to start a team of workers who will be available to go to patients' homes when needed). However, the police or an ambulance can be sent to take the caller to a hospital. This kind of action is very rarely taken. Even if some severe suicidal behavior has gone on, the therapist may decide that the real danger is past, and he may encourage the person to go to sleep or to go to a hospital by himself. For example, one woman called and said that she cut her wrists with a razor blade (a very inefficient form of suicide). After talking to her for an hour and noting that she did not seem to be weakening physically, the counselor decided against sending the police.

Only about twenty percent of the calls to the Suicide Prevention Line at the SPCS are actually concerned with suicidal preoccupations, although callers who do not discuss such problems may also have suicidal impulses. Some callers may make talking to the telephone therapist part of their lives rather than something to do in a crisis. These "chronic callers" may call back on over 100 occasions and may become so well known to the staff that the counselors wonder what has happened if no call comes in from them. Usually, the chronic callers use the service simply to ventilate their feelings rather than for support during a crisis. If chronic callers did not receive this kind of support, they might need to be hospitalized. The alternative of telephone therapy support is far cheaper and more pleasant for all concerned.

If the therapist decides that telephone therapy is not appropriate for a patient, there are a number of other methods he can use. He may refer the caller to a specialist on a specific problem (a physician, a lawyer, or Planned Parenthood, for example); he may suggest that the caller come in to the SPCS for face-to-face therapy; he may suggest that the caller contact a psychiatrist or seek therapy through a family services organization. In any case, the patient may always continue to talk to a telephone therapist when he feels the need.

WHY PREVENT SUICIDE?

In this discussion, we have assumed that the prevention of suicide is desirable. This attitude, which is shared by most people in our culture, is based both on the objective consequences of suicide (or its prevention) and on a priori beliefs. The most basic belief that applies here holds that the prolongation of life is always desirable. Life in itself is regarded as sacred. Reverence for life is a part of many religions; even when it is separated from theological tenets, it remains deeply ingrained in us. A murderer is looked upon with horror, and one who so denies the importance of life that he is willing to kill himself is considered by many people to be insane or basically evil. The taboo against taking one's own life is so deep that the subject is avoided in speech. The use of euphemism may extend even to distortion of the cause of death on a suicide's death certificate.

In addition to these deep-rooted feelings about suicide, there are many objective reasons for prevention. Persons whose suicide attempts are thwarted are often grateful for being saved and they shudder at the idea that they might actually have died. Those who call a suicide prevention center are clearly ambivalent about dying, for they are asking for alternative solutions to the problem. If a suicide is successful, considerable suffering may be experienced by the survivors. They are deprived of the companionship, protection, and often financial support of their friend or relative. In addition, they may experience great guilt and distress because they contributed to the suicide's problems or at least failed to save him. In groups where suicide is highly taboo, the family may feel disgraced. Children may be tormented by the notion that their parent's suicidal tendencies may have been transmitted hereditarily to them.

Probably one of the most important aspects of suicide prevention stems from the idea of suicide as the end of a gradual process. The suicidal person has many difficulties other than his suicidal behavior per se. The successful and permanent prevention of suicide involves correction of the problems that are leading the person toward suicide, thus making him a happier and more productive person rather than simply keeping him alive.

In spite of all these good reasons for the prevention of suicide, the question sometimes arises whether it is appropriate to try to prevent the suicide of a particular person. Many suicidologists would say that prevention efforts are always appropriate. Existentialists, on the other hand, would contend that suicide may sometimes be a healthy act. The existentialist psychiatrist Binswanger (1958), in reporting the case of his patient Ellen West, felt that suicide was the only healthy, free, mature, and responsible action of the patient's life. It was a time when she made a true choice and acted only in terms of her own interests, without her behavior being distorted by the influence of others. Most observers of suicidal people would not go so far as to permit suicide because of its existential advantages. Sometimes, however, a case may arise in which a person must constantly be followed and guarded over a long period of time because of his continuous interest in suicide. We must ask ourselves whether the minimization of the person's dignity and humanity through constant observation is not more damaging to the quality of his life as a whole than the possibility that his life will end in suicide.

Again, as people have different styles of life, each may have his own style of death. For some individuals, death by suicide may be the appropriate end to life. Finally, we must assume that some suicides occur on rational grounds and are (both subjectively and objectively) preferable to further life. Suicide is always one of the possible solutions for a problem and it may at times be the best one. Shneidman and his colleagues (1965) state that even severely ill persons should be discouraged from suicide because "while there is life there is hope" and because the guilt of their deaths will create a crushing burden for their loved ones.

In answer to the first point, however, it is rather rare that a person who, by all symptoms, appears to be approaching death is totally cured and returns to a normal life. As for the guilt of relatives, it would be more realistic for shame to be experienced by those who insist on forcing a kinsman to maintain an unwanted and painful life. Severe guilt over the suicide of a severely ill relative may be either pathological or deserved because of previous unfair treatment of the person; in either case, the guilt is not an event *within the life of the dying person,* who is the one we should be concerned with.

Perhaps we should realize that the quality of life can be more important than its quantity. There are times when people should not be subjected to prolonged agony followed by inevitable death simply on the grounds that "life is sacred."

BIBLIOGRAPHY

BINSWANGER, L. 1958. The case of Ellen West. In R. May, E. Angel, and H. F. Ellenberger, eds. *Existence.* New York: Basic Books, pp. 237–364.

SHNEIDMAN, E. S., FARBEROW, N. L., and LEONARD, C. V. 1965. *Some facts about suicide.* Washington, D.C.: U.S. Government Printing Office.

CONCLUSION

In much of the research we have discussed, we have been forced to conclude that no conclusion is yet possible. However, there are some facets of suicide that research has clarified. Here is a list of facts about suicide that research has supported.

1. Men tend to complete suicide, while women tend to attempt suicide.
2. For whites, middle and old age are the most common times for suicide, while blacks tend to commit suicide while in their twenties.
3. Cultural factors influence the suicide rate.
4. There is no evidence that any one drug works directly to cause suicide.
5. People who threaten or attempt suicide are more likely than others subsequently to complete suicide.
6. Suicidal people have generally disturbed social relationships.
7. Psychological tests are not good predictors of suicide, but behavioral indicators (like sleep patterns) may be.
8. Suicidal people tend to be rigid in their thinking and tend to think in extremes.
9. Economic depression is followed by an increase in the suicide rate, while war results in a decrease.
10. The weather, the phase of the moon, and activity of sunspots do not affect the suicide rate.
11. Suicide is more common in those who are psychologically disturbed.

The fact that these things have been ascertained gives support to the idea that suicide is no mystery, but is instead a human behavior that follows a set of rules. There is no question, however, that far more research needs to be done on suicide. It has taken people years to break away from their concern with suicide as a criminal act. It will probably be many more years before public opinion changes so that suicidal acts are no longer seen as shameful and as requiring concealment. Both these changes will have to be complete before suicide research can really move ahead: research workers will have to be willing to do difficult, tedious empirical studies, and the public information that is used in research will have to be trustworthy.

In the study of suicide, as in the investigation of other disturbed or undesirable behaviors, we fortunately have a source of information outside of research. That source lies in the large amount of clinical experience which therapists have accrued in dealing with suicidal patients. This kind of information is not "controlled" in the research sense, but it may give us valuable clues and a general feeling that can help in the understanding of suicidal behavior. To allow the reader to share in clinical intuition about suicide, we will quote some ideas about the development of suicide—ideas suggested by Norman Farberow and his colleagues at the Los Angeles Suicide Prevention Center.

"During a recent staff meeting at the Suicide Prevention Center, the question was asked: How would you make a suicidal person? Assuming you have free rein to do as you wished with a newborn infant, and disregarding genetic or constitutional factors for the moment, what would you do to guarantee that he would eventually kill himself at some time in his future life? At first taken aback, but then caught up to the task, the staff began to list the individual experiences and social and cultural conditions which should occur. In the former, he would be provided with personal experiences which would produce a self-concept totally lacking in feelings of self-worth or adequacy, and with constantly reinforced feelings that he is unlovable. A punishing superego filled with powerful feelings of guilt and shame and intense self-criticism for inability to reach specific standards would be fostered. Defensive mechanisms were to be denial and repression, with inflexibility the main characteristic of the thinking processes. Society's contribution would be values derived from primarily Anglo-Saxon American culture which would emphasize achievement and accumulation of wealth, and romanticize unrealistic love.

"More specifically, one would make sure that he had the wrong kind of mother and father, parents who would constantly emphasize for the child his ugliness and unlovability. The interactions between the child and his parents, especially his mother, would be programmed to produce deep feelings of inferiority and strong feelings of guilt. Warmth, contact, love, and support would be grudgingly given when young, and only when it would provoke guilt when older. Mother or father would assume credit for any accomplishments, and the only way he would get recognition or 'love' would be by being good enough to bring some kind of glory to his parents. Yet unhappily, no matter how hard he tried, he could never be good enough.

"But the picture is not yet finished. At five years of age, the father, a weak, ineffectual person, commits suicide, and the mother states flatly that the child had driven him to it. Within two years after, the mother places the boy in a foster home, thus succeeding in totally abandoning the child and making him feel responsible for having lost both his parents. At this point, the foster father, a big, masculine man, begins to exercise constant pressure toward masculine activities, such as sports, an area for which the boy is totally unsuited, having had no prior opportunities, encouragement, or experiences. The child strains under the two elements which dominate his psychic life, a demand to achieve and a foredoomed inability to attain. The foster mother would be involved with her own children and unable to devote any time to the boy. His real mother, on her infrequent visits, continually identifies the son as being so much like his father. The occasional moments of relief in school, in his gang, or in the childhood illnesses which he is suddenly given to, only serve to make his world more chaotic, inconsistent, and undependable.

"One potentially saving grace has appeared somewhere along the course of the child's life. He has discovered the fantasy world and escapes eagerly from the pressures of reality through dreams of admiration and acceptance. But even here the subculture in his foster family assists in the eventual outcome, for it believes in a hereafter which includes the attractions of paradise and glories of heaven for those who strive hard enough. Thus, death is not an ending; rather it is a transition point toward an eternally happy existence" (Farberow, 1970, pp. 45–46).

BIBLIOGRAPHY

FARBEROW, N. 1970. Self destruction and identity. *Humanitas* 6: 45–68.

INDEX